also by Michael Phillips
The Seven Laws of Money

also by Salli Rasberry
The Rasberry Exercises

HONEST BUSINESS

HONEST

BUSINESS

A Superior Strategy for Starting and Managing Your Own Business

Michael Phillips
and Salli Rasberry

Clear Glass Publishing Company · San Francisco
Random House · New York

Grateful acknowledgment is made to the following for permission to reprint previously published material:

Heyday Books: Material from *The Ohlone Way: Indian Life in the San Francisco–Monterey Bay Area* by Malcolm Margolin, © 1978. Heyday Books: Box 9145, Berkeley, California 94709. Reprinted by permission of the publisher.

Harper & Row, Publishers, Inc.: Specified excerpts from pages 649, 651, 652 and 654 from *Management: Tasks, Responsibilities, Practices* by Peter F. Drucker. Copyright © 1973, 1974 by Peter F. Drucker. Reprinted by permission of Harper & Row, Publishers, Inc.

Library of Congress Cataloging in Publication Data
Phillips, Michael, 1938–
  Honest business.
  Includes index.
  1. Success.   2. Small business.   I. Rasberry,
Salli, joint author.   II. Title.
HF5386.P584   658'.022   80-6037
ISBN 0-394-51779-2
ISBN 0-394-74830-1 (pbk.)

Manufactured in the United States of America

98765

Dedicated to Cynthia, Scott and Laura Phillips, Sasha Freiberg, Bob Bell, Sam Gnaizda and all our friends in the Briarpatch

PREFACE

This book deals with a superior strategy for business that emphasizes openness, community and extensive access to information.

Many of our friends and associates have expressed doubt when told we were writing a book about honest business, feeling it is impossible to maintain an open and honest business and keep food on the table. Honesty in business is usually equated with failure.

The image of the cigar-smoking, secretive, cutthroat executive is the popular stereotype associated with American business. Successful businesses are portrayed in film and other media as mysterious, insensitive establishments existing solely for big profits.

It is customary in most businesses to use deceptive pricing, deceptive advertising and to keep wages of most employees secret unless the government or a union demands that it be open.

While the concept of honesty in business expressed here is revolutionary, the practice is not. In Chapter 17 we describe four men whose honesty created great businesses.

We believe that when personal honesty is incorporated in business practice the resulting business has the best chance for survival. Myth to the contrary, honesty has strategic superiority in the business marketplace.

What Is Honest Business?

The concept of honesty is made clear by thinking about your friends who are extremely honest and comparing them in your mind to friends who aren't. The difference is the "absence of fraud or deceit" among those who are honest.

When we deal with extremely honest friends we have a high level of certainty that their statements will be accurate and direct and that their promises will be fulfilled. Less honest people make statements that are inaccurate, vague or confusing. Though people may intend to be honest, their words must be compared to their actions. We compare what people say to us with what they do; we also compare what they say with their behavior toward other people.

Francis, a store owner, had a dispute with a customer. She told him that her store had the most liberal refund policy in the area for the past few years. Since he didn't believe that, she arranged to phone him the next day after investigating whether her claim was still true. Fran did check, found that the facts supported her and phoned the man back as promised.

The customer, who had been rude and belligerent when he first talked to Fran, was kind and apologetic when she phoned. He himself had checked other stores and found less-favorable refund policies, and he was also pleasantly surprised to be phoned by a store owner who he knew was terribly busy. He sent flowers to apologize for his rudeness and became a loyal customer.

When we translate our people-based understanding of the word honesty into being honest in business, the concept of "absence of fraud or deceit" remains equally valid. An honest business is one where we know that the statements, implications and promises we hear about the goods and services offered are accurate. Furthermore, we know from the business's actions that instances of confusion or misunderstanding on the part of the customer are remedied promptly and carefully. Abe Lincoln's reputation for honesty comes from the tale about his job in a store where he ran for miles to return some pennies he had overcharged a customer.

Honesty in business is more difficult to evaluate than honesty among people on a personal basis. We can compare the statements of individuals with their actions to determine fraud or deceit. Evaluating a business is a different matter because a variety of people are involved with a diverse set of "intents." To evaluate a business's honesty we can evaluate the aggregate intent of the people in a company. With openness we can compare their many statements with their actions to determine their honesty. Openness and secrecy are opposites. Openness exposes fraud and deceit. The less openness the more room for dishonesty to function.

For example, in most restaurants where excellent food is prepared by proud chefs, customers who appreciate the food are welcome to enter the kitchen and thank the chef. When this unique tradition of openness is practiced patrons get a chance to learn a lot about the nature of the restaurant, especially its cleanliness. In a few so-called "excellent" restaurants, patrons are kept out of the kitchen with reasons ranging from "you'd be in the way, it's too busy back there," to "our insurance doesn't permit customers in the kitchen." It's easy for customers to imagine that these "closed" restaurants are hiding either a dirty kitchen or dinners prepared from frozen food shoved into microwave ovens by teen-agers. Their secrecy is assumed to cover up the intent to deceive the customer.

Being honest is a superior way to do business. Being open about business is important, beneficial and necessary. We know that excellent restaurants can survive without letting customers see their kitchens; what we hope to show is that similar excellent restaurants that are open will do much better.

A closed, secretive business is not automatically dishonest, but we have found that keeping honesty secret is self-defeating. The authors have worked with over 450 open businesses in the past eight years. Of these less than 5 percent have since failed. Eighty-five percent are still in business. The rest have been sold, the owners married, died, retired or otherwise changed their lifestyles.

As you read through this book, you will find that several businesses are referred to repeatedly. This is because we want to show the connection between the real operation of an honest business and the variety of qualities that fit together to make it work.

CONTENTS

Preface   ix

1. What Is Business?   3
2. Tradeskill   11
3. Love Business   23
4. Focus Your Energy   29
5. Service   37
6. Small Capital   43
7. A Complete Idea   53
8. Go Slow   63
9. Study the Books   71
10. Open Books   83
11. Community   93
12. Paying Bills Promptly   101
13. Management   105
14. Fun   123
15. Short Bits of Advice   127
16. The Four Illusions of Money: And the Nonmoney Truths They Hide   169
17. Four Honest Men Who Changed Business   175

Appendix		183
A.	History of Business	183
B.	Honest Business in the Broader Context	193
C.	Facts About This Book and the Authors	199
Index		203

HONEST BUSINESS

Closed antique store with Art Nouveau lamp. Frustrated pedestrian is Bob Gnaizda

1·WHAT IS BUSINESS?

The grocer spraying fresh vegetables before sunrise in the wholesale market, the psychiatrist talking to a bank salesperson about a computer service to bill clients, the telephone company employee leaving three telephone directories on your front steps, the spinner selling woolen hats at the county fair, the receptionist answering an incoming call at the local Red Cross office.

These people are all involved in business.

This chapter defines what these people have in common and how business is differentiated from other things that people do, such as having sex, eating, singing and parachute jumping.

In very personal terms, business is the pervasive activity in each of our lives that connects us to the large number of people who provide us with food, clothing, fuel and most other goods and services we don't produce directly for ourselves. Business consists of our interaction with these people, an interaction that usually is independent of friendship or social ties. Weekly, each of us deal with scores of people in business, as we constantly exchange money, goods and services with those who provide us with important necessities. That network of connections is business, and each exchange of goods and services is called a transaction.

Transactions

A "transaction" is the specific exchange of goods and services, but we've expanded the term to mean that *all parties to the exchange have maximized their individual desires*. We all tend to think of business as the exchange of goods and services for a price. We often don't see the broader context, that all parties have voluntarily carried out the exchange and agreed upon its terms. It is this mutual agreement that has important and useful implications.

Imagine being an invisible witness to a simple transaction at your local flea market as two people negotiate a price for a 1947 General Electric toaster. The seller cleared out his basement and feels the toaster he found wedged between some old bottles and books is worthless. Still, he has some lingering belief that it might just be a collector's item. The buyer runs an antique business in a trendy neighborhood and believes that with a little work she can sell the toaster at her standard markup. They settle on $15 for the toaster and each feels happy with the transaction.

Another example of mutual agreement is a dentist taking an x-ray and filling a tooth for an agreed-upon price of $60 for a first visit. Both parties have arrived at the amount of money to be exchanged for the dental service by independent evaluation of their desires. The dentist wants to charge a price that covers his or her costs, that will allow room for the variation in problems with dealing with people, will cover the overhead costs of the office and staff, and will yield the annual income that he or she wants to earn. The patient wants a tooth filled at the lowest price possible commensurate with the level of professional skill desired, and wants appropriate concern for his or her emotional needs.

Neither of the individuals in the exchange will continue the relationship if many nonmonetary elements of the transaction are not satisfactory. If the patient feels the dentist is unskilled, inconsiderate, inattentive or otherwise disinterested, the patient will seek another dentist. Similarly, if the dentist feels that the patient in unnecessarily fussy, likely to complain regularly about dental work or drinks too much alcohol, the dentist is likely to decline future dental service.

The transaction is the context in which the exchange of money for services occurs. Michael uses the following experience to illustrate that it is within the context of mutual satisfaction that transaction occurs.

"Muldoon, the owner of an art gallery, and I were recently involved in a traditional business transaction. I had purchased five pieces of art fifteen years ago, for $2,300. I wanted to get rid of them at any price as I was simplifying my life. Two of the pieces were by a deceased artist who had shown exclusively at Muldoon's and never had another show. Two other pieces were by an unknown who, unfortunately, had remained so. The fifth piece had been painted by Muldoon, himself, who has sold very little of his own work. All in all, I considered I was not a successful art investor and was anxious to sell.

"Muldoon and I bargained for about half an hour, and settled on $5,500, payable to me over three months. I could have considered myself a very sharp bargainer to have made such a profit over worthless art, valuable only to Muldoon. It turns out he might well have considered himself the shrewd one, as he sold his own piece a short while later for $15,000. Actually, we engaged in a transaction and each of us was happy with our exchange."

Each exchange we encounter may have a whole range of considerations that are not directly involved in the exchange, but which are central to it. These considerations customarily include repair service that we expect with products, refundability of defective merchandise, respect and courtesy from sales personnel, sanitation in food and health businesses, and many others. Business is made up of transactions, not just exchanges.

Fraud and braggadocio get in the way of good transactions. Fraud occurs when you buy a mahogany table in a bazaar and get home to find out that three of the legs are pine. Clearly this is not a transaction as we've defined it, since your desires no longer match the price you paid for the table. You have been cheated by someone in business. An exchange, not a transaction, occurred. Businesses can survive on exchanges for some time, but in the long run it is transactions, not exchanges, that keep businesses going. There are mothers who abandon their children, automobile drivers who get killed in accidents, television sets that don't work, but the definition of mother, driver and television set are independent of the exceptions that occur in daily practice. Cheating does occur in business, but it doesn't define business.

Braggadocio is a more serious factor in confusing our understanding of transactions, because it occurs frequently in business. We often hear of people who have made a fortune at someone else's expense. The antique buyer who bought the toaster for $15 and later sold it at a handsome profit might brag about her shrewdness in taking advantage of the "poor suckers at the flea market." This kind of bragging is not uncommon and promotes the popular image of a businessperson as shrewd, insensitive and unfair. In this instance, though, a transaction did occur because both parties can happily view their own success in meeting their desires. The seller might have gone home and said to his wife, "I did great today, sold that broken toaster to some fool for fifteen dollars, the one that had been useless in the basement for twenty years—a few years back Goodwill wouldn't even take it." Bragging is a very common one-sided view of transactions, but the transaction occurred because all parties found the price that gave them the most satisfaction.

A Series of Transactions

Business must be repetitive, otherwise it is a fluke, an accident or a singular event. When we sell a house in one neighborhood to move to another, and don't do something like that again for five years, we are not in the house buying/selling business. We have sold a house when we were moving.

Henry Dakin, a wonderful friend, kindly allowed us to use his computer and a room in his home to write this book. After a year of writing we felt we were imposing on Henry's generosity. We mutually agreed to a small hourly rate of $3 for using the computer. At the point when we agreed on the payments, Henry was only renting the computer to us and using it the rest of the time for his own work. It was not really a business. However, accommodation became business when Henry rented it to other friends and it became a genuine business for Henry. The IRS *might* have accepted the first arrangement as a business, but it certainly would do so after more than one rental agreement existed.

We could cite many instances where a person engaged in a transaction once, or even a few times, and most people would not consider it a business. The significant element underlying our common-sense understanding is that business requires deliberateness, intent. Without a series of transactions we can mistake the activities for accidents, frivolity or experiment. The series allows us to observe intent.

Regularity Over Time

A small antique store on Pike Street in Seattle had an interesting Art Nouveau lamp in the window, but the store always seemed to be closed. We asked someone next door about the antique shop and were told, "People keep asking us; the guy who owns it comes in a few times a month, unpredictably, for a few hours; it must be just a tax shelter for him or something." Without regularity there is no business; instead the activity is a toy or a game. Even at weekend flea markets there are "regulars" who are in the flea market business and "amateurs." People who come regularly, even if it is just the first Saturday of the month, are considered to be in business.

Regularity is a central element in the definition of business because every business requires a community of buyers. (This will be discussed in detail in Chapter 11, where the concept of "community" is explored.) For a community of buyers to exist, it is necessary that they have some form of common activity. Regularity of the business is often the minimal form of commonality that exists. In the case of the closed antique store, we were a nascent community because of our interest in the lamp in the window. We could have become a part of that store's community and would gladly have signed a guest register for mailings about Art Nouveau lamps if only we could have found out when the store was open. The same is true for flea markets. Someone like ourselves, with a casual interest in Art Nouveau, would not go to flea markets regularly, but when we did, we would go to the seller who had a table of Art Nouveau pieces on display. It would be their business to buy from the one-time amateurs and resell to us. They are in business. They would be the ones offering the regularity that would make it worth our while to visit the flea market at all.

Nonretail businesses also need regularity. A business conducted over the telephone could be like the flighty antique store if the telephone is never answered, if the business is not listed in the phone directory, if it has no answering service or answering machine, or has an answering machine that is out of order for weeks at a time. Common sense would say that such a business was out of business. While the business activity itself may be totally erratic, as with companies that fight oil well fires, or with private detectives, there must be some regularity to allow customers access, even if it is a telephone where one can leave messages that are picked up every three days. Regularity allows buyers to find the business.

Business is also distinguishable from hobbies and traditional housework. A hobby does not involve repetitive sales on a regular basis, with concern for assets. The same is true of a husband or wife who stays home to clean the house, cook, take care of children and handle the associated community relationships. These activities are not good training for business. In the same way, the home auto-repair person, or the houseworker who sews clothing for friends, does not learn appropriate business skills from these activities; the hobby or housework only offers experience in the specific skill of repairing or sewing. Neither of these involves transactions over time and thus cannot be a business.

The most marginal case of regularity might be traveling gypsies who stitch ripped awnings for a living. They can't be reached by buyers in need. While they are certainly in business, they have no regularity from the buyers' point of view. This is a case where the service required of the business is itself irregular—you only need it when your awning's torn. Within that realm the business has some regularity. If people with awnings know that gypsies pass through their own town about twice a year, and that the awning's damage would be clearly visible to a passing gypsy, they might wait to repair it until a gypsy came by. If the rainy season were coming, they probably wouldn't wait.

Concern for Assets

People who gamble regularly are not in business unless they support themselves with their earnings. The concern for assets is the common-sense test. The person who makes a bundle and then loses it a week later is a gambler. Making a living at it makes one a professional gambler, or someone in business. In that case, the steady accumulation of assets equal to the liabilities of food, clothing and shelter is the visible evidence of being in business. Such people don't often keep records; the cash in their pocket, the clothing they wear (including jewelry) is the measure of their effectiveness in their business. Their savings and net worth are the direct reflection of their business.

The tax authorities use the concern for assets as a test of business. If a company shows a pattern of steadily dwindling assets it is not considered a business. If someone says they are in business but ends each year with fewer assets than there were in the beginning, there is immediate doubt as to whether they are, in fact, in business, and the burden of proof is theirs. This becomes a tax issue because people often claim that losses on one "business" can be deducted from the taxable earnings from some other activity.

Concern for assets in business does not necessarily mean increasing them. The environment in which business operates is often unpredictable, and assets may be lost. Preservation of assets during an inflationary period is often a reasonable strategy resulting from the more fundamental "concern for assets." Concern for assets is a distinction that separates business from charity. A person or an institution that methodically gives away assets is not in business; however, businesses do exist for the purpose of helping individuals and institutions to distribute assets.

Concern for assets in business is regularly reflected in accounting and record keeping. This is in contrast to other activities where records are seldom kept.

Summary

Business links us to a large number of people who provide us with goods and services. Business is a series of transactions which tend to be frequent and regular over time. Business also includes a concern for assets that is reflected in accounting and record keeping.

Bess Bair (lower right) *performing as Rosie Radiator with four of the Push Rods*

2·TRADESKILL

Tradeskill is the most important attribute of anyone who is in business. We use the word to describe the qualities that make one person more effective than another in starting and running a small business.

Tradeskill is not the same as "business ability"; there are people who possess tradeskill who are not in business and there are many business people, including top managers, who don't have tradeskill.

A skill, just like carpentry or computer programming, tradeskill is necessary to start and maintain a small business. If you possess a lot of tradeskill you can start and run a number of different kinds of businesses easily; if you have a modest amount, one business may be a lifetime effort. If you lack tradeskill altogether, we suggest you find someone to work with who does have it—the attributes are described in this chapter.

Parents and Childhood Experience

In comparing the qualities of the successful small-business people we counsel with those whose businesses fail, we see a consistent pattern. Usually the person who successfully starts and runs a small business either had a parent or close relative who had a business or, in a few cases in which the parents were not the source, they had significant business experience themselves before the age of eighteen.

The children of taxi drivers, greasy spoon restaurateurs and dentists have a very good chance of succeeding in business. Children of teachers, bureaucrats and soldiers don't. A child who worked in her father's drugstore selling sodas, or in his mother's bookkeeping office doing ledgers, has a good grasp of how business works and can respond, intuitively, to business advice. All the unspoken, invisible issues of business are subtly communicated to children, and no amount of schooling can fully take the place of that process.

If this was a test in the *Ladies' Home Journal*, you would receive eight points for having two parents who were in business for themselves, six if one was in business, or four if you helped Uncle Morris in his drugstore. Having been in business for yourself before the age of eighteen would be worth five points. You can make it with a score of five or more. Some people have scores of ten, and find business a completely natural part of their lives.

When parents and relatives don't provide the milieu for tradeskill to naturally develop, individuals can create useful business experience for themselves. We can't pick our family, but business experience before age eighteen can broaden our options. The variety of early businesses that people with tradeskill have considered useful ranged from newspaper routes to selling plant seeds during summer vacations to running fireworks stands in July. The important criterion is sustained energy: running a lemonade stand for two weeks one summer would not help much.

Many parents may not be in business but still wish to encourage their children to develop tradeskill. Michael felt that way and made an offer to his children to pay half their fare to anywhere in the world if they would earn the other half. His fifteen year old took the challenge and learned to weave pillows and spin yarn. She made the pillows on a piece rate basis, and spun the yarn on a per pound rate basis. Within a month, she was earning over $6 an hour with her new craft skill. Seven months later she was able to spend a month in Singapore visiting her grandfather. Selling what she makes at crafts fairs is an easy matter for Cynthia, and her confidence in her ability to take care of herself is evident. She will have tradeskill all her life.

Rasberry says, "While working on this chapter, I am obliged to take a realistic look at myself as regards tradeskill. My parents were not in business for themselves, and neither were any close relatives. I didn't have a newspaper route, and only once sold Campfire Girls cookies. I am not interested in working nine to five, or even twelve to four, or working *for* anyone else. What I do is trade energy when I can, and crochet garments from my handspun, naturally dyed wool. I *could* make enough to support myself, the market for handspun yarn and woolen products is there. But I don't have tradeskill. Looking at my work pattern, I have always worked *with* others, as I am on this book, for instance. I believe that if I want to make wool work my business, I must take on a partner with tradeskill. Otherwise I will keep my crochet work as a hobby and some other partnership possibility will present itself."

People about to go into business for themselves might want to make a similar realistic appraisal of their tradeskill. Our society makes it so easy for anyone to start a small business that few people question their own tradeskill abilities. There are several alternatives to consider if you don't have tradeskill: you can go ahead (and probably fail), you can find a partner, get special training or find a boss.

The worst consequence of failure in starting a business will only be having to go back to work for someone else (if you don't lose other people's money). If you learn the lesson of how difficult business is, you will no doubt appreciate working for someone else.

You may decide to find a partner to join you in your business who has the appropriate tradeskill to complement your strengths. Make sure it's someone you like and trust. Talk to that person as frankly as possible about your strengths and weaknesses and encourage him or her to do the same. Write down everything about your partnership agreement that you can think of so that the terms of your business arrangement as well as your working arrangement are absolutely explicit. This is important even with very close friends because the more open the communication, the less chance there is of misunderstanding and difficulties that might damage your basic relationship. (See "Partnership" in Chapter 15.)

You can decide to get special training and develop tradeskill. This usually means working for someone else in a small business and accepting increased responsibility until you are effectively running the business. You may have to work in such a situation for a number of years before you are effectively prepared. At present there are no schools that offer tradeskill training.

You can find another person or persons who have tradeskill and work for them, choosing someone who can effectively use the talents that you have to offer. Bob Schwartz, who runs the very imaginative and important School for Entrepreneurs in Tarrytown, New York, asked about ways to identify potential entrepreneurs from among the many applications he was processing. Since entrepreneurs need tradeskill to succeed, Michael suggested that the best measure would be the letters of recommendation that were submitted by applicants. The ones with the most letters from independent business people, regardless of social status, would be better able to use the school than those who had letters from teachers, family lawyers and political dignitaries. Bob says that this criterion has been reliable.

Regardless of whether or not they have tradeskill, people who have spent many years in nontradeskill work find it difficult to make a shift to self-employment. Michael's father, Wendell, was a rabbi until the age of forty-five, when he decided to go into business for himself. For the next ten years he tried the import business, ran coin-operated movies, had a coffee vending-machine business and even had a supermarket concession with horses that went up and down, excited children astride, for a dime. All his business ventures were marginal with an occasional glorious fiasco. Eventually he gave up to go back to work for others as an anthropologist and college administrator.

When Louie Durham retired from his position as Director of the Glide Foundation in San Francisco, he decided to go into business for himself. For four years he attempted to run a variety of businesses and finally went back to work for someone else. Louie is an imaginative organizer, particularly capable of working with other creative people. The years he spent toying with small-business projects was a clear lesson to him that his talents need to have an institutional framework. He realized he didn't have sufficient tradeskill and so linked up with others who could use his talents. He is currently Dean of Students at the Institute for the Advanced Study of Human Sexuality.

Tradeskill Attributes

Tradeskill is the cluster of attributes that allow people to effectively start and run a business. The people who have this set of attributes find them extremely valuable in their business lives. These attributes can be boiled down to four: persistence; the ability to face the facts; knowing how to minimize risks; and being a hands-on learner. Each of these are necessary elements of tradeskill, yet none of them individually are sufficient for business success.

Persistence consists of being willing to keep trying something long after your energy is used up, long after your enthusiasm has waned and certainly long after other people have lost interest in helping you. The people who can't make it in business are the ones who give up easily or divert their attention from the long, hard parts to do the easier, more glamorous parts. Everyone who succeeds in starting and running a business has the attribute of persistence.

An example of a person without persistence is Phyllis. She had a part-time business selling a book she had published, but wanted to start a small retail shop that would sell dolphin products exclusively. Phyllis had enormous energy, a wide variety of skills, warmth and intelligence. Each time we've run into her over the past three years, she has asked for advice about her proposed dolphin business. We advised her to work as a sales representative for some of the products she wants to sell and learn which are popular and who buys them. We've advised her to talk with sales reps who carry the lines she is interested in, to get sales figures on picture books that have been published about dolphins, and lastly, to talk to the owner of a local store that sells frog-related products, exclusively. She hasn't followed any of our advice because it requires persistence.

Each time we talk to Phyllis she asks us to evaluate some new plan to raise capital for her proposed store, or asks us to look at some storefront as a potential site. She usually tells us about important people who are interested in her idea. So far, she hasn't followed up on the obvious suggestions because they deal with the less exciting parts of business—the footwork, the grindstone jobs, the things that are integral to business. There are always hard, boring, dull parts of business that are behind the easy, exciting parts.

There is another aspect of persistence that people often overlook. Hookers have it. Several years ago Michael was involved in a small project attempting to retrain street prostitutes. Most of these were working women who generally had a five-minute attention span if there was no danger or excitement around. Michael tried to help them work as telephone switchboard operators, something that doesn't require a long span of attention, but sitting still all day didn't appeal to them. On the other hand, no matter how many times they were put in jail for prostitution they were always right back at work the same day they got out of jail. That was an incredible persistence in the face of constant opposition, and necessary in their business.

Facing the Facts

Being willing to let go is of course what "facing the facts" is about. It involves the ability to learn constantly from empirical evidence and the willingness to change your behavior when the weight of the evidence tells you to change. This attribute of tradeskill is distinctly different from the quality in people that leads them to change their behavior because of new ideas, convincing arguments, pride or whim.

The sense in which we use "letting go" does not refer to quick responses to everyday pressures or to blowing in the wind. Rather it refers to a willingness to let go of belief systems that is only found at a very high level of functioning. It refers to letting go of one's personal patterns and beliefs. It is pragmatic behavior, and it is difficult for many people.

An example of facing-the-facts behavior would be a potter who works with a variety of glazes and clay shapes; the ones that come out of the kiln in the desired form are the ones that are duplicated even if they don't appear to make chemical sense, and the experiments that crack are rejected.

A good example of facing-the-facts behavior in business was Stewart Brand's nurturing of the *CoEvolution Quarterly* (*C.Q.*). The number of pages, the format and the cover changed significantly with each issue as Stewart explored his own style. Some issues sold well on the newsstands, some hardly sold at all. The future looked fairly glum by the time the fifth issue was due because of cumulative losses and slow subscription growth.

Michael suggested that Stewart's first priority was controlling costs. He suggested setting a limit on the number of pages and reducing the amount that contributors were paid for articles. Stewart had started *C.Q.* with the idea that his page count should fluctuate with the amount of material pertinent to each issue, the traditional practice for most quarterlies. He had a large background of experiences to weigh in making his decision, in addition to the experience of producing the first five issues. If he took Michael's advice he would have had to discard some of the ideas he had started the quarterly with. Limiting the number of pages required great emotional wrestling for Stewart, but because he has superb tradeskill, and thus the attribute of facing the facts, he decided to set a limit on the number of pages at 144, which has remained to this day. Limiting the number of pages gave him a vital parameter within which to work, leaving him freer to experiment with several methods for reducing costs and increasing sales. Stewart did not reduce the pay for his contributors because the facts supported his policy of paying well for superior work. The content of *C.Q.* was excellent. While he was aware that his contributors would have worked for less out of loyalty, he realized that exploiting their good will would be self-defeating in the long run. The *CoEvolution Quarterly* has evolved to become the American magazine with the most interesting words per dollar of cover price.

Minimizing the Risks

Risk and tradeskill are surprisingly connected. People with well-developed tradeskill minimize risks! If forced to choose a gambling game they would favor roulette where the odds are close to 50/50, and avoid slot machines where the odds are worse than 25/75, although the payoffs are higher. They would avoid gambling in the first place, and own the casino when they have that alternative. We call this attribute "casino-istic." The casino owner minimizes risk in two ways: first by offering many different games and getting the insurance protection that comes from the variety of sources of income; and second, by only taking a percentage of each game rather than participating directly in the gambling.

When giving business advice, we usually throw in one or two suggestions where the payoff is large but the risk is visible (like a big increase in price). We've never seen a person with well-developed tradeskill bite.

When looking at new businesses most tradeskill people we've known were very open about looking at completely new ideas and strategies, but when the implementation period came, they methodically went about reducing the risk. They find fall-back plans and alternative solutions in the event the main thrust of their venture doesn't work. They constantly think of alternative uses for the equipment they are using, or for subletting their location if their plans don't work. People with the casino-istic attribute carefully decide at what point and under what circumstances they would cease taking a risk in their business.

Bess Bair, a beautiful and joyful tap-dance teacher, is a perfect example of this. To others it might have looked as though she was taking a big risk when she decided to borrow money for a new dance floor for her studio at a time when she didn't yet have the students she needed to pay the costs of the loan payments and was flat broke with no assets except a talking parrot. In fact, her high casino-istic attribute led her out into the neighborhood to get commitments from other dance teachers to use her studio if she didn't get enough of her own students. Bess then got the loan, and, of course, this dynamite teacher got a surplus of students.

Hands-On

People who succeed in starting and running small businesses have the hands-on attribute very visibly before they start a business. They learn by touching and doing. They are hands-on people who gain confidence in their decision making by participating in all the processes that relate to the decision. Such people pay close attention to details. They carefully look at contracts before signing them. They read legal notices that come in the mail and they invariably go back to look at the new wiring that the electrician put in before the wall is sealed up.

It is not unusual to discover that people with this attribute find it difficult when their businesses grow large and have many employees, because they are not prepared to delegate responsibility. This is a case where a tradeskill attribute conflicts with a management skill.

Dick Raymond, who is one of our close, beloved friends and teachers, has some of the other attributes of tradeskill, but isn't a hands-on learner when it comes to business. He started a business called One More Company and raised money for it by using his eloquence, charm and charisma. With part of the money raised he paid himself a well-deserved salary and rented an office. He then spent the rest of the money and much of his time looking for the right secretary, hiring bookkeepers, interviewing potential partners and once got a computer projection of his products' future sales. He worked like this for nearly a year with numerous employees joining the company. Yet the mail wasn't regularly answered, the product wasn't promptly shipped and almost no sales revenue came in from the magazine ads on which much time and money had been spent. Dick seemed to have a managerial conception of business where things like answering letters, following up on sales leads and shipping the product out every day were for specialized personnel. Dick didn't have the hands-on approach to his business.

Fortunately for the investors, he had persistence. He kept waiting for a person with fully developed tradeskill to come along. One finally did, Paul Hawken, founder of Erewon Food Company in Boston and a tradeskill master. Paul agreed to take the job and save the company, if he could fire Dick and everyone else.

For six months he did all the work himself, answering the mail and phone, doing the bookkeeping, sales and personally shipping the product every day. He didn't hire anyone to help him until the sales revenues would cover the cost and allow him to start repaying the loans. Paul, at the time of this writing, has sold the company for nearly a million dollars and Dick was a major shareholder at the time of sale.

General Notes on People with Tradeskill

The following are some characteristics associated with people who have good tradeskill that are reflections of the four basic attributes.

The hands-on attribute of tradeskilled people sometimes means they like to carry things out, to get in there and do something, much more than they like to talk about it; often they are not verbal at all about how they do business. Most people we know with tradeskill like to do their own books and they pay daily attention to financial material. This seems to be a direct result of the hands-on learning attribute, since the books give a hands-on, comprehensive feeling of the business.

Sometimes their face-the-facts behavior over many years enables tradeskilled people to see customer reaction more clearly than other people can see it. To outsiders, they seem to make a gut-level connection between investment and return on investment. They know that putting in some new windows, or buying a slightly better machine, will increase their revenue by more than enough to pay for it. Don Tatum, who came from a prominent business family, put a large garden in the back of a building he remodeled, which he rented to a bakery/coffee shop. That garden really helped the bakery/coffee shop to be a successful business which, in turn, attracted other good businesses into the arcade in the front of the building. Don knew when we talked to him in the early days that using the space for a garden rather than another business would be the greatest return on that space. This is the end result of superb empiric development.

A reflection of this same face-the-facts way of learning from experience is seen in the tendency for people with high tradeskill to get crusty in their old age and impatient with someone else's attempts at things they're tried and failed at themselves.

The persistence attribute seems to lead to an awareness of the slow process by which things occur in the world and to the realization that time increases the likelihood of success. People who face the facts understand that wisdom is gained by the constant reevaluation of life experiences. People with this attribute have an expectation that better decision-making information comes with time.

Business people who minimize risk know that over time random activities have an average value and that decisions based on an average are far more reliable than ones based on chance or on a single event. Such perceptions honed into a day-to-day practice are, in themselves, a successful strategy for dealing with business. These perceptions and practices are passed on through families and developed empirically in the teen-age years.

Summary

If you are going into business, it is necessary for you to have a cluster of attributes called tradeskill, or to join an individual who has it. Such an individual is persistent, responsive to factual evidence for decisions, minimizes risks and learns by touching, doing and getting their hands into everything. They most likely had parents who were in business for themselves, or they learned business in their teen-age years.

Bahauddin Alpine (at right) *and partner Sherman Chickering delivering some* Common Ground Directories

3 · LOVE BUSINESS

In order for your business to start, grow and flourish, you must love it. There are many reasons for loving business: the chance to meet a variety of people, to make a lot of money, to influence others, to travel, to change the world. To love business is to make a total commitment to its needs, which requires dedication of your time, attention and considerable passion. This love of business is vital. Our experience is that you *have* to love business to put up with the trials it brings you.

As a rule of thumb it takes two years to either start a new business, or two years to take over and learn an existing business. This two years is a minimum.

These two years of trials include boredom, insurmountable barriers, baffling dilemmas, hopeless conflicts and bewildering isolation. It takes a deep-down love of business for most people to put up with the difficulties and sometimes agonies of those first two years.

It is much harder than most people expect to run a business, and it requires much more time and energy than most people assume at the outset. If you don't have strong motivation to struggle, you might be happier not going into business at all.

One of the worst hurdles that business presents is the unexpected deluge of endless daily problems. Bill was a plump public school teacher who loved ice cream. He decided to go into business, located a small storefront, put in a counter and started to sell ice cream a month later. After five weeks of working every day and dealing with the neighborhood kids, bills, licenses, sales tax, theft, messy floors and the phone, he disappeared. His roommate sold the business to someone else.

A second example, of an imaginative, energetic redhead who loves machines and has an extraordinary ability in designing and machining, is Tom Conlon, who was manufacturing wind-powered generators in a large warehouse. In his first year, he found sales were easy and he thought he had production of his first seven generators under control. He felt free to try new designs and focus on the fancy machining equipment that he had leased. He lost track of his production schedule, and it wasn't long before his customers were angry and a deluge of financial pressures beset him. Some of his orders were eight months behind schedule. The pressures increased, personnel problems appeared and finally an outsider was brought in to run the company as Tom slowly eased out. Tom found that setting up a production line to manufacture generators was a far cry from turning out seven prototypes. He loved the design and mechanical things he was doing, but didn't love the business end of it enough to cope with the daily deluge of problems.

In most cases, business is terribly complex and unexpected. It will creep up behind you and really shake you sometimes. To endure some of these "shaking" periods, it is essential to love business.

On the other hand, it is very common to hear someone who has been in business for a year, who from our vantage point is a complete novice, say, "Business is really easy, I get pretty bored at times." The point where people become bored is the precise point where more new and constructive energy is most needed in the business.

Kathy is a warm, generous woman with a Ph.D. in medical science, who, by herself, published a small paperback book about nursing. Though she felt she had the distribution process down pat, in fact she had done very little promotion for the book, with little marketing, no effort in reaching the libraries, no reviews or excerpts in magazines on its subject. The book had sold only five thousand copies and Kathy had really just begun to explore its potential. Yet, at the time we saw her, she had invited us in to talk about doing a new book, on a grander scale. The trouble was that she had become bored with promotion of the first one and was ready to move on, even though she had failed to reach her audience.

Janet, an innovative cook, ran a vegetarian soup kitchen located in a storefront in a downtown environmental center. Even though her cooking was spectacular, after a year her business was dragging, with luncheon customers ranging from five to fifteen people. Janet was bored, and it showed in her lack of customers. She began fantasizing about branching out into the catering business and starting work on a cookbook, which was to include several hundred vegetarian soup recipes. Luckily though, at about that time, in order to promote the soup kitchen, she gave a few elegant dinners with unique themes. As a result, through word of mouth, her lunchtime business nearly doubled the second year, and she became totally immersed in the cooking she truly loved. Based on her experience of the first year, she might have completely lost her basic business if she had branched out into other areas as a result of boredom.

Loving business is necessary to overcome the barriers to new business survival, such as the flood of problems and boredom. Having a passion for business helps to get you through the difficult periods, and it also helps improve the business. Our close friend, Bahauddin Alpine, is a twinkling-eyed formed lawyer, international marketing expert turned Sufi teacher and publisher. His *Common Ground Directory* takes ads from growth and spiritual groups, and is distributed free in four counties in California. Twenty-four hours a day, Bahauddin is aware of his business. His love of business is magnetic. We've gone out for tea in the evenings with him and always, on the way out, he'll check the bulletin boards to see if there are any new groups he hasn't heard of yet. If there are, he'll write their names down. Even late at night, coming home from a class, he'll stop to write down the name of a spiritual group that he sees posted on a telephone pole. He carries copies of *Common Ground* to distribute wherever he finds a likely spot. His mind never stops thinking of appropriate places to distribute the directory. I remember one time when he went back to leave a pile of his directories at an acupuncturist's office because he realized the people had time to read while they were being treated.

David Copperfield also has this passionate love of business. David publishes a health magazine in Santa Cruz called *Well Being*. Everything David does and loves ends up in his magazine. He writes about his garden, emphasizing healing herbs because of their relevance to the interests of the magazine; he put in a solar-heated hot-water system and discussed the health effects of the water. His passion and his business are integrated, making his personal life both positive and rewarding.

Rudy Hurwich was founder of Dymo Corporation, which was bought by a Swiss company in 1978 for a large sum. Rudy grew up in Chicago, participated in his family's retail clothing business, and later developed an aluminum foil company. When aluminum was scarce during the Korean War, he moved into the unit packaging business, which allowed him to look at many other businesses. Six years later, he found the product that became the Dymo label machine, which Rudy nurtured into a diversified $300 million company. Now Rudy spends much of his time helping friends and interesting people with their businesses and gives enormous amounts of time to nonprofit projects that are new and imaginative. He is loved by all who know him for his generosity, warmth and wisdom.

The following is excerpted from a conversation with Rudy, which he later reviewed.

"I love business. For me, it is a palette to do my art, just as a painter would use a palette of oils to create paintings. Business is my art. A business transaction where all the parties are happy with the outcome, a new venture where the public gets a useful product or service, are all fun for me, and emotionally rewarding.

"Many of the business people I work with find what they are doing is also fun. Occasionally there are people who don't love their business or have fun at it. Often they are either doing poorly and blame others for their problems, or the business they are doing was something they chose as the lesser of several evils (such as working for someone else).

"The fun I've found in business comes from all levels of activity. It includes the long-range planning, strategizing and predicting in situations where you don't see the results of your efforts and vision for five to ten years. It includes the intense days-long negotiating sessions where we work to find a solution that will satisfy all the parties involved. The excitement is working with people, studying their psychology, seeing how they interact and how their value systems influence their behavior.

"I find this excitement in nonprofit business as well. In nonprofits, the communication needs are much greater than in conventional business, and this adds to the complexity. Most nonprofits pay their staffs less than the market, so the difference in wages are really contributions by the staff of their time. They do it because they get additional rewards from their work. Therefore, in a nonprofit, where you want the staff to get the additional rewards, you have to know what it is they want from their jobs (recognition, status, accomplishment). To find that out and integrate it into the operation requires more communication. The challenge is fun.

"Helping people start and manage businesses is exciting. People who do well at it have a unique talent and I respect their skills. Some people do wonderfully at starting a business, others are best at management. In my case, I found that my skills were best used at Dymo when I still had a hands-on feeling about the business; up until sales were $70 to $80 million. From then on, it was hard to spend even a half hour with a member of my staff without feeling the pressure to go on to the next decision that needed attention. At that point, the depth of interaction with people was no longer as rewarding for me, and another kind of manager was needed. That point where the founder no longer has a hands-on feeling for the company is at a different point for different companies, depending on the person and the line of business."

Summary

Loving your business is a necessary ingredient for its success. Business presents a constant barrage of problems, demands, challenges and long periods of boredom. Loving business is the source of strength for persisting.

Frances Peavey of Simple City Systems humorously assembling a chair

4 · FOCUS YOUR ENERGY

"I want to expand my tofu kit business and start tofuburger restaurants around the country, just like McDonalds."

"Now that we have finished our book, we want to get other people's books so we can start a distribution business and get our book better distribution."

It's possible that some extraordinary person with a great deal of energy and highly developed tradeskill could make either of these ventures successful, but most humans who are struggling to make their businesses work should be wary of dreams like these. Business requires that you set an appropriate focus.

When Larry came to us, he had more fantasies than just the plan to expand his business into a tofuburger chain. In addition, he was setting up an import business to bring commercial tofu-making equipment from Japan for the burgeoning tofu business around the United States. He was already producing small wooden tofu box kits, that retailed for $13 and were used to make tofu at home. He also had a new lover who was taking lots of his time.

We felt that Larry hadn't even started to develop his tofu kit business, which had only been operating six months, to its full potential. We advised him to give all of his attention to that business and totally exclude all other projects (except his lover). He listened to part of this advice and dropped the plans for a chain of restaurants, but he kept the import project. His main problem was his failure to focus his energy on the primary business, which desperately needed attention. Instead, he diverted a lot of energy to the tofu-equipment import project. The consequences were bad.

The reason Larry had trouble is that the import business was a radical departure from his primary kit business. Tofu kits were being marketed to the public through a large number of natural-food retailers. This business is significantly different from the business of importing commercial tofu equipment, which involved selling products to a few specialized food manufacturers who were just getting started and needed lots of information, training and support service.

After eighteen months of juggling both businesses, Larry was forced to take a much-needed vacation. Totally exhausted, he was virtually unable to supervise the tofu kit business while he went away, and there was nothing he could do with his import business, which he now wanted to sell. Larry was stuck; the import business was just barely alive, limping along. He had reached the stage in the import business where there was an enormous amount of paperwork to do regularly, a mass of translation from Japanese to English that was needed on equipment instructions. There were a few meager sales each month and many prospects who needed a great deal of attention which resulted in a high rate of telephone soliciting expenses.

The final blow came when another importer, operating in Los Angeles, became active in the tofu equipment business full time. What kind of monster did Larry have on his hands? He either had to let his incipient new business fold, or let it take all of his energy to the exclusion of his primary business. The chances of finding a person with enough knowledge to manage or buy the import business were probably nil, and if he or she did exist, they would be able to start such a business on their own. The tofu box business suffered severely from this lack of focus on Larry's part, and at this point the tofu kit business is nearly dead.

Larry's focus should have been on his primary business, not on unrelated tangents or grandiose schemes.

Lenore and her bookkeeper Anne were two spunky women who had published a book themselves and wanted to go into the book distribution business. It was a warm sunny day, and we were sitting in the backyard listening to them. Their position seemed logical enough; since they were going to distribute their own book, why shouldn't they use the same amount of energy necessary to carry one book around to stores and represent ten other books? They could take a percentage markup on all the books in the process.

We asked them if they wanted to be in the distribution business, or whether they mostly wanted better distribution for their own book. "Our book," they said.

There are more effective ways to obtain better book distribution, we suggested. Had Anne and Lenore gone into the distribution business, for what were really unrelated reasons, they would have started off with several strikes against them. It would have been hard for them to be objective about the relative importance of their own book, and they might easily have ignored market forces that supported the value of some other book in their line. Even worse, had the business succeeded for some unexpected reason, they would have found themselves working full time in a business they did not really want to be in. We've met other people in that situation, where they longed to go back to the thing they wanted to do in the first place.

One alternative to distributing a line of books themselves would have been to take their book to an established publisher and negotiate a distribution agreement that would allow them to supplement the publisher's promotion efforts with their own. Or, they could publish it entirely themselves, and incorporate the requirements of distribution into their whole business.

An example of someone who engaged in this kind of integration is Bernard (Bear) Kamoroff, who wrote and published *Small Time Operator*, an excellent book on accounting and related problems written for small businesses.* Inside Bear's book there are mailing forms that allow the reader to order additional copies. Bear does his own order fulfillment, mailing the books out of his home in the country, and in that way he gets revenue from the mail order part of the business. By doing this himself, he makes about 20 percent more per book. He loves the handwork involved in this part of the operation, because it is similar to his accounting experience.

Bear also does his own book promotion, giving interviews to the media, sending out occasional flyers to bookstores and doing workshops about his subject in neighboring towns. In addition to his own efforts, his book is listed with Bookpeople, a large West Coast distributor that handles orders for small self-publishers. Bear's book is in its sixth printing at the time of this writing, with forty thousand copies having been sold.

With forethought, Lenore and Anne could certainly follow Bear's example. Book size, planning for review copies and order forms inserted

---

* Available at $6.95, from Bell Springs Publishing, Laytonville, California, 95454.

in the book are part of the design considerations that go into a success-ful independently published book.

In the two cases described, the advice about focusing your energy is based on distinguishing what business you are in from other seemingly related functions. For Larry, importing commercial tofu equipment is much different from manufacturing and selling home kits to retail stores; for Lenore and Anne, publishing one book is much different from run-ning a book distribution business.

What kind of similar business line would not mean a loss of energy? Jungle Ball foods, a group that makes organic, high power candy balls, added some different flavored balls to their line, a natural evolution for their business.

Shoepatch, a company that makes and sells material for patching the soles of shoes, particularly runners' shoes, added some black goo to their clear goo line of products without diverting energy from their main line.

Don't Focus Too Narrowly

Focusing your energy also means allocating your energy over the long haul of the business to the appropriate areas of concern, as the following example illustrates.

Sheldon wrote a book called *I Love Radio*. It is a magnificent book. In it he listed all the radio stations in his area, and carefully reported on what he found out about how each station runs their news depart-ment. He checked on what wire services they used, how many reporters and desk staff they had, the times of the news and talk shows, including foreign language news broadcasts. Sheldon was a gentle but awkward man who, for many years, had been a junior-college teacher. He planned to do a series of these books on radio, with each book dealing with differ-ent subjects ranging from music shows to religious programming.

Sheldon had done the entire *I Love Radio* book by himself. He did the writing, the research and the typing. He took courses to learn how to do the layout and photos, which he shot himself. He took courses in printing, and then printed five thousand copies of the book with his own savings. After sending out a few copies to radio stations and getting very little response in the form of orders or offers of promotion, Sheldon gave up.

When we met Sheldon, we were excited about the book. We gave him the necessary advice on what to do to get it distributed, but it was too late. Sheldon had expected the world to beat down his doors, and it hadn't. He knew he didn't understand marketing, and he hadn't taken a course in it, but by then he was out of energy. He went on to find other pursuits.

We often think about what kind of advice might have been helpful to him. He is in this chapter because he faced an energy focusing problem. Although he did focus his energy on one business, something else was missing. It was missing in a way that is not uncommon to other people starting out with great sincerity in a new business. He knew what he wanted, which was to publish this wonderful series of books for people who loved radio as much as he did. But he never got past the marketing of the first one.

When we visited him, he was well on the way to finishing the copy on the second volume in the series, but he wouldn't print it until the first one got some strong response in sales, which it never did. Was it the image of all these books from his series sitting on a shelf that was the dream motivating Sheldon? Did he forget to include an image of ten thousand people buying and reading it? If he could have formed a clear enough image in his own mind of what he was doing, he could have focused his energy on completing the process. He didn't just want a series of books on a shelf, because if he had, he could have produced just one copy of each, with the same amount of money and energy that it took to do the first one, and then xeroxed them and put nice bindings on them, as Otto Swartz III, another friend of ours, did. It is clear that his image of the books missed the image of marketing them; the whole business was not in his mind, so that he focused only on part of it—on less than the whole. The opposite of Larry, who focused on too much, Sheldon focused on too little.

The two examples that follow are of women who have carefully balanced the issues of focusing their energy in their business, and who have done a wonderful job.

Betty Dodson is an artist and a spectacular advocate of the joys of sexuality and masturbation. She came to us several years ago, wanting to discuss publishing a book called *Liberating Masturbation*. We told her that she would find the most joy for herself in publishing her own book, and that included the art, the layout, the printing and the distribution. Since Betty constantly travels around the United States visiting her friends, lecturing and giving body/sex workshops, marketing would be simple. Betty, who fully understands the idea of personal fulfillment through work and leisure, grasped the suggestion wholeheartedly. She spent three months doing the book, and had a wonderful time. She then got her friends all over the country, who loved the book, to help her distribute and sell it. The book sells for $5, and Betty, as author, artist and publisher, gets $3.10 per copy. At the time we are writing this book, Betty's book has sold a hundred thousand copies, which has kept her busy distributing it for four years, and has been a good source of income. Because *Liberating Masturbation* related directly to what she was doing—teaching women and making sensual drawings—it absorbs her excitement and is beautifully integrated into the whole message of her life. Her whole being, including self-pleasuring and sexual satisfaction with masturbation, is worked into her book business.*

Fran Peavey organized a group called the Co-Counseling Community in the San Francisco Bay Area, which today has many thousands of people involved. In co-counseling, people help each other by applying simple counseling principles in their own one-to-one counseling situations, and avoid the authoritarian and expensive approaches used in standard psychoanalytic models. Fran was also a key organizer in the attempt to save the International Hotel, where a group of Asians and Filipinos fought for years, with the help of many friends, to save their low-income housing from the bulldozers of high-rise office building developers.

Fran's extraordinary organizational talent wasn't wasted when she started her own business. She opened a very small retail store called Simple City Systems, on an out-of-the-way street in San Francisco. Her merchandise was novel, including all types of furniture and fixtures for city living, with special emphasis on book racks that could be put up and taken down in a few minutes, as well as tables and lofts that could be disassembled and moved easily by one person. She aimed at serving the needs of renters who move frequently.

Fran had a business background. Her father used to show all his children how a farm he owned worked, and how others in the area nearby operated. She opened her store a month before her announced grand opening, in order to iron out all the problems of a small space and hard-to-order merchandise. When Fran officially opened, she did it with spectacular publicity, and business was booming from the first few days. With her taste of success so immediate, she did a natural thing, which was to begin to expand.

Being an experienced organizer, Fran expanded in a very wise way, focusing her energy and that of the business. Anticipating that people

* *Liberating Masturbation*, Box 1933, New York, NY 10016.

who buy urban furniture are also interested in urban gardening, she began four related businesses. One handles the sale of bees, chickens and worms, items for urban gardening that aren't easily available. Another business designs and sells rooftop gardens that are made and installed in modular form for easy removal. The third, "bumpkin" service helps people from faraway towns who come to San Francisco to buy furniture. One of Fran's employees takes them to the wholesale furniture showrooms, helps them choose what they want, then drop ships their purchases to them in their hometown. The cost savings for the "bumpkin" over their local store price is enough to pay for the trip, and the business utilizes skills Fran's employees already have. The fourth business is a mail-order catalogue of the many unique items Fran has found.

All these businesses are synergistic in a very real and direct way; the employees work interchangeably on all of them and Fran's superb organizational skills fit into her imaginative venture perfectly.

Summary

Focusing your energy in business means clearly understanding what business you are in, and setting boundaries on your activities that are not so broad that they encompass things that will divert you, and not so narrow that something that is the lifeblood of the business is excluded. With good focusing, all the new elements of the business should work together to stimulate it as it grows and changes.

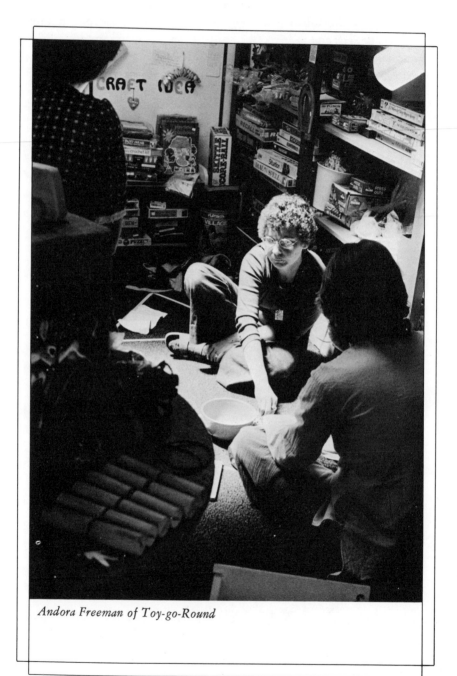

Andora Freeman of Toy-go-Round

5 · SERVICE

There are many reasons why people are in small businesses. If their main reason is to serve other people, the business and the founder have many advantages.

Being involved in business can be one of the most exciting and rewarding parts of our lives, whether we deal with a big business or a small, privately held company, corporation or partnership, or a company that is nonprofit. The reason that business has such a potential for being rewarding is that it is a very special way that people can serve each other.

"Service" is the conscious act of offering our talents, resources and support to other people. For us, service is one of the most important criteria we have in choosing what we do with our lives. Most of us who find service to be so important do so from a very deep inner sense. In those rare moments when our ego and our daily concerns are stripped away, we find in that calm, gentle core a generous fountain freely offering its abundance to others.

Business offers a variety of opportunities to serve for all kinds of people with many different values. This differs from the common religious forms of service, which are usually limited to cloisters, monastic living, teaching, welfare aid, medical assistance, missionaries and shelters for the aged. Business may include many of these, but it also extends to others, allowing a unique form of service for many people who have nonsectarian values. In business we can serve people quietly without the subtly implied "I am helping you" quality that often surrounds religious "service." To us, that is truly extraordinary.

The master carpenter serves people by fully and thoroughly doing the job. When each nail is carefully driven, when each corner is perfectly fitted, then all of us benefit. Similarly, the builder who hires the carpenter to build structures that are aesthetically and socially valuable, and who fully utilizes the talents of the carpenter, is also serving. So is the financier who aids the process by openly counseling the builder on ways to operate that include the needs of the community in which they all function.

Our friends Bob Gnaizda, of Public Advocates, and Gary Near use their law practices to bring public interest cases before the courts. They choose their cases from among the social issues they believe will enable them to best serve the community. Both of them frequently ask themselves, "What am I doing right now in my practice to serve my community?" When approached by a new client, they ask, "How will my time spent on this case be of service to many people?" Many lawyers probably do this.

Businesses with employees and management who frequently ask such questions discover that new ways of doing business often evolve and that the fundamental personal values people wish to have in their work are more likely to be satisfied.

Carole Rae, an accomplished weaver, often asks herself what she is doing to serve people with her art. This questioning has led her to pay close attention to her dealings with employees. She sees her relationship to them as one of teacher, guide and example, dedicated to helping them become better weavers so that they can expand their own artistic skills and serve even more people. To ensure that the relationship between client and artist is extremely clear (so that the whole process will have value to her client), she spends many hours with the people who are commissioning her work to better understand their needs. This helps the customer understand and value their own role in the creation of a new piece of art. Most important, Carole offers her talents as broadly as her energy allows. She voluntarily designed an impressive billboard for a community church; she loaned one of her tapestries to a new women's bank and two others to a composer for use as a stage setting for one of his performances. In every way she looks for ways to serve others; and as astute readers will have noted, many of these acts of service have wonderful benefits for her business. Lending tapestries has increased the number of people who see Carole's work, while her attention to each client means more referral business.

Andora Freeman and Joy Hecht have a toy recycling business (Toy Go Round) that grew out of their desire to serve other people. Andora is an energetic woman who was a schoolteacher in Chicago for many years. After raising two boys, she decided she could afford to start a business. Her partner, Joy, is a calm, hard-working mother who grew up with five brothers and sisters. Their business, recycling toys, is of real benefit to their community. The sellers benefit because they are paid in cash for toys they would ordinarily give away or discard. The buyers benefit by getting more toys for less money. The community benefits from the saving of resources that would be used to make new toys. Andora and Joy make a profit by taking a percentage from the toys they sell.

Andora and Joy have translated their overall view of the business into day-to-day specifics. By constantly questioning how they can serve people they have developed many new ways. For example, they deal personally with each person who brings in toys to sell by phoning them after the toys have been evaluated and the market prices estimated. They take the necessary time to tell people what price they propose to mark each toy, even though some people bring in many boxes of toys, and other people simply leave one box without even asking the sale price. They expend the energy because they want to make sure that the desires of the toy-seller are completely understood before the toys go on the shelves for sale. Andora and Joy help each customer to understand how the business works and to see what value other people find in various types of toys. They often counsel people on choosing toys for a child, telling them if a toy is unsuitable for the child in question, and advising them not to buy a certain toy if they have found it inappropriate for that age child. Andora and Joy mark toys if pieces are missing, and put distressed portions of toys in view. This careful attention to the needs of the customer has a number of direct benefits: reduced complaints, long-term loyalty of customers, and it helps the customers, themselves, to evaluate the usefulness of the many toys that are on the market. Many of their clients are young people and in those cases they are extremely patient because they see it as a wonderful chance to teach children how business work. They see it as an important way to empower children, giving them a way to earn their own money by selling the toys they no longer want.

Morrie Kadish, who took up marathon running in his fifties, has been operating a very conventional paint contracting business for more than twenty years. He employs union painters, which allows very little flexibility in how his business can operate. But since Morrie works to serve people, he constantly finds new ways to help.

When he estimates jobs for people he is very open with his information, regardless of whether the information he gives leads the customer to pay more or less for the job. He refuses work if the potential client is painting on rotted, wet wood, or covering up shoddy undercoats or blister with paint in order to make a fast sale. He tells people that a lower-priced light color paint will last longer in the sun than a more expensive, darker color. In many ways he demonstrates that his first priority is to be of service to his customers. It's wonderful to do business with Morrie. He was one of the very first painting contractors to hire blacks and Asians, over much resistance from the local unions, because he sees his business as a service for those who want to work. Years later, when minority hiring became more commonplace, Morrie had the best trained and most loyal minority workers.

"Hey, wait a minute," some readers may say. "There are business people who don't have service as a priority in their work and still do all right."

Of course, how else could we explain the large number of businesses that have unpleasant employees, dirty environments, long lines and repulsive advertising? These businesses thrive for a while even though the owners are not at all interested in service. Aspects such as convenience, warranties and monopoly outlets can help outweigh negative considerations.

A business that provides goods and services with goals unrelated to the business itself or without desire to serve has a very good chance of failing. More than eighty out of one hundred don't even last three years.

Wonderfully, many businesses do operate on the principles we describe in this book, and they succeed. This is certainly the case in the small-business network that we have worked with, where the failure rate is about five out of one hundred. The following are four examples of new businesses that practice service, which are part of this small-business network:

The Pickle Family Circus, a group of twenty loving souls, includes clowns, tightrope walkers and a six-piece jazz band, and is a business in which all the participants, and occasional helpers, love what they do. The Circus performs for community organizations, sharing the gate revenues and making money on midway booths. The community group is responsible for the promotion, and the Pickle Family does the circus, in a symbiotic relationship. As the Circus's fame grows, so does its ability to help community groups.

One of our favorite examples of a person dedicated to service is Huey Johnson, who has a passion for conservation of land. Huey worked for many years for the Nature Conservancy, during which time he became very skilled at buying property for the Conservancy at a much lower price than a public agency would have had to pay for it. He would then resell the land to the public agency at a price that was lower than the agency's appraisers would customarily offer. Huey had the advantage of offering tax benefits and immediate cash to the land sellers. When Huey started his own organization, the Trust for Public Land, he used the markup that came from his skill in buying and selling to cover his operating expenses. His approach has been so successful that Trust for Public Land is continually training people nationwide who are now able to save land on a massive scale.

Information on Demand is a computer- and library-based research firm run by Sue Rugge. Sue's staff has developed great expertise in the use of the many information data bases stored in computers around the world. Using terminals in her Berkeley office, she is able to scan many millions of data files to find information that customers want. Once the relevant article or report is located, a staff librarian finds the original document and makes a copy of it from local library records. It is very inexpensive. Sue serves clients in many unusual ways. One customer is a man whose wife has cancer. Sue's firm regularly provides him with the latest research articles in areas of medicine that relate to her illness.

Tom Smith built a home for himself and his family in the mountains of Lake Tahoe. The house was one of the first standard contractor-built homes to use an effective, passive solar heating/cooling design. The house has become a business for Tom, who trains contractors in passive solar building techniques, publishes pamphlets and booklets for the do-it-yourself market and acts as a consultant to architects and individual homeowners around the world interested in duplicating his success.

Summary

Serving others is a natural vehicle that business offers. Many forms of serving people are available in the business world. When service is a primary goal of a businessperson, the chances for success are greatly enhanced.

Tom Hargadon in Finnegan's Wake

6 · SMALL CAPITAL

When you start and run a business with the primary goal of serving people, you will be more effective by starting with minimum capital. Minimizing your capital requires maximizing other business components such as quick response to the market, attention to details, and innovation.

The idea of starting with small capital is opposite from the prevailing view of most graduate schools of business, and from the advice almost universally given by small-business writers. The most commonly stated reason given for the failure of small businesses is that they are under-capitalized.

Nonsense! Undercapitalization is the prevailing excuse for insensitivity to the real needs of the market. Too much capital is often a more serious problem than too little, as the following example indicates.

Fred was a small-business person who went into the natural-foods business because his daughter convinced him it was a good business. Fred's astuteness in hiring a good manager in his first store, and letting him run it the way he wanted, resulted in a very successful enterprise. Fred's success led him to open a second store across town. With the profits from these two businesses, Fred decided to expand into another "hippie" business, though Fred, himself, was a hard-drinking, loud-talking, cigar smoker. He bought the space next door to one of his grocery stores and had it renovated by fine carpenters to match an elegant hip restaurant in Sausalito that he admired. The restaurant was remodeled with beautiful wood sculpturing and fine detailed trim. Renovation cost over $300,000. He then opened it as a luncheon restaurant offering a mixture of vegetarian foods, lots of meat dishes, sugary things and espresso. His fine new restaurant was in a neighborhood with a large vegetarian population, natural-food eaters and feminist organizations. A nearby vegetarian restaurant that was a little on the scuzzy side, and that offered a $1.50 curry special, was usually packed. Fred's, with a $2.65 sliced ham and avocado sandwich, was usually empty. The restaurant in Sausalito that Fred copied really thrives because of a large tourist trade and an elegant singles crowd, a far cry from the folksy, feminist clientele in the neighborhood where Fred opened his restaurant. To add insult to injury, when Fred decided to do something about his empty carpenter's palace, he invested in a fancy new $100,000 renovation that included a bar.

The addition of a $100,000 bar didn't do anything to attract the health food or local feminist foot traffic. After two years of staying open with very little business, Fred put in another $150,000, and turned his place into a singles' bar and grill, which is now doing "all right."

Fred has lost money because he had to pay interest on the $550,000 in direct capital improvements that he put into his business, and also had to pay an additional $100,000 in wages during the two stagnant years before he found some customers.

Fred had too much capital. Had he started with very little money, instead of pursuing his expensive theories, he would have been forced to respond to the needs of the neighborhood or to go out of business.

Businesses that start with little capital are forced to pay close attention to what is going on around them and keep awake to what is happening in their environment.

Attention to Details

People who start their business with small capital usually have high personal labor and emotional stakes in their business, and consequently they respond immediately when they find a small change that will be beneficial.

Frequently, when visiting a small business, we'll suggest some change in the floor plan, display or pricing. People who started with capital, and agree with the advice, will do it immediately. However, business people who have plenty of capital, even though they agree, often do not take corrective action for a long time.

Jack, a burly ex-parole officer, opened a pottery store on a street with high pedestrian traffic. Business was quite slow, but Jack had plenty of savings to carry him another six months, through Christmas, so he was pretty fat catty. We made three suggestions that he clearly understood and agreed with. One was that he post small signs, in many places around the store, encouraging people to touch the pottery, since that was one thing that made his way of running the business unique. Another was that he change the front window display from hanging planters to cups and teapots. The planters made it look too much like a plant store from the street. Lastly, since the store was set back from the street, we suggested a large, five-foot, attention-getting urn or ceramic sculpture near the sidewalk. Jack eventually put up the signs and replaced the planters, but it took nearly four months—not much attention to details. Too much capital is like too much food, it makes people lethargic.

Having a business with too much capital discourages attention to market pressures. Much more subtle market forces are easy to ignore, even for businesses that start with modest capital. One example comes to mind that probably wouldn't have been detected promptly had the business not been so tiny and close to the edge of survival. Michael called the subtle force in this case "conceptual smell."

Skin Zone sold scents and lotions. Sherry, the tall, independent owner, had found some colorful plastic toilet seats which she liked and she hung them near the ceiling in her tiny, crowded, two-hundred-square-foot store. They seemed "soft" relative to conventional toilet seats, and her store was directed at "pleasure and comfort." When a friend of hers saw them, he commented that there might be an emotional conflict among customers. As he put it, "Toilet seats are to toiletries as dirty is to clean." Sherry polled a number of customers and, from the looks on their faces, she knew her friend was right. She took the toilet seats down.

In a small store, everything is noticed and the effect of each new line has to be watched very carefully. In this case, Sherry had very quick feedback about the subtle but real market forces that affect a store. This helped her avoid a mistake. Her small capital situation helped her friend notice this potential problem, and tell her, and small capital prompted her to respond seriously.

Rasberry encourages and supports the Manfredie's pottery shop in the small country town of Bodega, where she lives. The owners had an accountant figure their income taxes and were very satisfied with his service. Imagine their pleasure when he called to let them know that he had been thinking about their tax return, and remembered an additional deduction worth 20 percent that they could take. The man was actually the local agent of the national H & R Block chain, but his small business out in the country really depends on his kind of care and concern for customers.

Every small-capital business depends heavily on the way each customer is treated, and consequently looks closely at how they serve people. Aren't you shocked when you witness small errors or rudeness at neighborhood stores? The consequences are often far out of proportion to the incident.

At a typical small, neighborhood grocery store, the average customer purchase is under $3, but most customers have yearly totals that exceed $150. Offending a customer in a situation where the money outlay is $3 can affect a much larger chunk of business. A small business should be better able to comprehend and respond to the long-term effects of each customer interaction than a large business.

Dan knows the importance of each of his dental patient's visits, although a $15 visit is only part of a family's average $150 yearly dental expenses. Daniel started his dental practice on a low budget, with equipment bought at an auction. Many of his first patients were young, and often came referred by free clinics and dental schools. He gave them all his complete attention on every office visit. From this attention and care for each patient grew many family loyalties and a successful practice.

Innovation

Innovation is one of the most interesting benefits derived from starting a business with small capital.

Carole Phillips runs a restaurant within a restaurant in Santa Cruz, called Suzanne's After Hours (she is no relation to Michael). Suzanne's is a fine restaurant that serves wholesome, fresh food of Northern Spain in a lovely white cottage. They stop serving dinner at 10:00 P.M. After they have cleaned up, Carole comes in and runs her After Hours Restaurant, complete with a guitar player or flutist, until closing time at 2:00 A.M. Both restaurant operations benefit from the multiple usage of the facilities. Another Santa Cruz restaurant uses the same principle for three shifts, the luncheon crew being different from the dinner and post-dinner crews. The neighbors love the variety and novelty of it.

Gary and his Circus of the Soul Bookstore started out by sharing space with Oz's Roommate Referral Service. Gary got the good foot traffic generated by Oz's business, and Oz's clients had something interesting to look at while they were waiting, during busy times, for someone else to finish looking at the listings of housing to share.

For many years, Stewart Brand has let his layout and typography staff use his workplace and tools for their own client work when his magazine was not in production. One benefit, to him, has been the new talent that has been drawn into his *CoEvolution Quarterly* from the other projects that have gone through the shop. Also, according to Stewart, skilled people are on hand when a sudden need for one turns up.

Benefits of Small Capital

If your capital is small, you need your community to help you, and that need spurs useful feedback as well as free promotion. You also have advantages in dealing with employees, and gain from reduced, long-term overhead.

The Sacred Grounds Coffee House started with the help of many friends of the two women owners. Their friends worked all three shifts for very little pay. For a coffee shop, the participation of friends was very good for business. The network of friends of the friends who were working at Sacred Grounds rapidly helped build a customer network.

The same experience was true for Raskin-Flakkers Ice Cream and for Second Chance antique store. In both cases, the owners had their friends and members of their religious communities work in their store and help out with renovation and decorating. Very quickly, other community members began to feel that this was "our" store.

Certainly every immigrant in business understands this point, because immigrants have to use their community network to survive in the hostile environment they usually find around them.

Connie's is a West Indian restaurant run by a robust, outgoing, happy woman who has strong political views about racism and the problems of black people in America. For many years, Connie has regularly held performances in her restaurant to benefit various political groups like the Black Historical Society. She also has put on various testimonial dinners for people like Malvina Reynolds, the late folksinger and composer. Connie cooks delicious dinners, and gives all the profits of these benefit dinners to charity. When hard times came for Connie in early 1975, and business was very slow, her friends loaned her money, got her some free sources of food, helped her negotiate a more favorable lease with her landlord and came in to help with the dishes. She made it through those times and quickly repaid the loans.

Employees

Better employee relations is probably the most obvious benefit of starting a business with small capital. Though it may seem a contradiction, the fact is we have found that in an open business, offering small wages initially attracts employees who have commitment and passion for the business. These qualities can't be bought and they are often strangled in the comfortable and unchallenging surroundings of a well-financed new business. Employees who work for you, not for high salaries but for love of the business, tend to live simply and to place a high value on a work situation where what they believe in is appreciated and nurtured. Employees with passion work hard and concern themselves with all the details of the business. They care about the customers and offer good feedback about minute, day-to-day events that subtly shape the direction and form of the business.

Long-Term Overhead

Long-term overhead is automatically lower if you start with small capital. The "overhead" of a business refers to the minimum expenses that cannot be cut. Even without salaries, there are still rent, utilities, maintenance and similar expenses to contend with. One of the expenses that never goes away is the cost of the money initially invested in the business to get it started. This original investment is called capital. The future overhead of the business is your lost interest on the capital (if you borrowed capital, then it is the real interest to be paid on those borrowings). The higher the original investment capital, the more the business has to generate to cover the interest costs.

Starting with small capital will allow you to survive longer and be more competitive in a small market. You can use this advantage to pay better wages or offer lower costs. Fred's restaurant and singles' bar, used as an example at the beginning of this chapter, cannot be as competitive in the price of their services as the Acme restaurant down the street. Fred probably has a monthly interest cost of $4,000 or more, where Acme's monthly interest cost is under $500.

What Is Small Capital?

A good working definition of small capital is any amount that is much less than a conventional businessperson feels comfortable starting a business on. Most small-business advisors talk about having enough money to pay slightly lower than normal wages for eighteen months of business, even if the minimum amount of business is transacted. Many of our business friends started with two months' cash reserves and plans to move in with their friends and take no wages if the business grew too slowly. For one couple with children, it meant reducing costs by taking in a boarder, and bringing their young child to the store each day to avoid childcare expenses.

Small capital does not mean foolish cost cutting that hurts the business. For instance, many retail stores need a large stock of inventory to make people feel that their prices are low, and a wide range of sizes to fit most customers. If the new business is too small to meet the real needs of customers, then the customers won't come back.

Should you accept financing for starting a small business from banks or the government? No. If you don't start with financing from a bank or similar institution, the worst that can happen to you is that you lose your own money and time, and the money and time of others participating directly in the business with you. Then you and your friends go back to work for someone else. However, with debt from a legal institution to deal with, it is another situation. That kind of debt doesn't go away so easily, and it is usually an emotional burden that wasn't worth going into business for in the first place. In most cases, these issues aren't very relevant because you can't get a bank or similar loan unless you have sizable assets to be used as security for the loan in the first place.

Knowledgeable people might ask, at this point, about financing the business after it gets going and begins to need new capital to support its growth in inventory or equipment. Classically, this is the hardest point in time to get a conventional loan, so that's the time to borrow from the friends and community who participate in the business in the first place, because they clearly see and feel the growth that warrants the new capital. In some cases, financing of equipment is possible. That can make sense since the worst that will happen is that the equipment will be taken back to the supplier if you go out of business.

For more discussion of financing, see Chapter 11 on Community, and Short Bits of Advice (Banks).

Summary

Starting a business with the minimum amount of capital will force a business to be more attentive to the needs of the marketplace and the community it serves. It will also be more innovative in marketing and in reducing costs, more likely to find conscientious, loyal employees, and most of all, the business will be able to survive in a smaller economic niche. This last benefit results from lower overhead, which reflects reduced interest costs on the initial capital.

David Chadwick at the Green Gulch Greengrocer

7 · A COMPLETE IDEA

One of the most exciting aspects of business is starting with a new idea.

Such beginnings are precarious because it is rare for a new idea in business to succeed at all, much less survive for any great length of time. The way for a business to have the greatest chance to succeed with a new idea is to keep it whole—to conceive and execute a complete idea.

Communion Restaurant is our favorite example of taking a complete idea and making a successful business. The following account, with slight modification, is taken from *The Briarpatch Book.**

COMMUNION RESTAURANT

If a conventional restaurateur were to describe the Communion Restaurant he or she would probably say in tones of incredulity: "This restaurant isn't to be believed; they've done every single thing wrong.

"First they opened it in the wino section of town; second they have enough space to seat sixty people but the tables are so far apart they only handle forty people at a time; then there are all sorts of special oddities." Such as no smoking, *no talking,* no shoes in the part of the restaurant that's Japanese style and no buspersons; when you're done eating you take your own dishes to the kitchen and put the cloth napkin in a bag. There are no paintings on the walls, no music, and most of all no cashier. The cash register is an open cigar box where you make your own change.

That is incredible and that's not all. The Communion serves only one kind of meal: Indian food—chapatis, curry, rice, yogurt and a current vegetable; you can eat as much as you need. The people who run this restaurant originally charged 80 cents for all this when they opened,

* New Glide Publications, 330 Ellis St., San Francisco, 1978.

then when they found they were making too much money, lowered it to 60 cents and after eighteen months in business raised it to $1 so they could save money for their next venture.

The six people who started this business began with $5,000 they saved from jobs as construction workers. For that amount of money virtually no "going" restaurants could be bought. So for $3,000 they bought a lease in one of the worst wino neighborhoods in the city in a store that had a refrigerator, steam table, stove and some formica tables. The monthly rent was $200. The rest of their $5,000 was used for remodeling. All work was done with scavenged lumber and their own labor.

They cut the stove in half with an acetylene torch to make it more useful for the Indian food they serve, built their own chairs out of ply-wood and woven strings, and rebuilt the rectangular formica tables into square and round tables with wooden tops. (As they explained, "What side would you choose to sit on? If the table is rectangular you have to have a preference, so you create comfort for one person and discomfort for another . . . that is why our tables are only round or square.") Everything that was bought or built was based on the number of diners who could be comfortably served by two people. Once that was decided, it determined the number of tables and chairs, the size of the pots and the amount of kitchen area.

One of the founding members, a new arrival from India, found that "this country looks like a huge supermarket. You turn on any TV chan-nel and most of what you see is about food. I spent my first three months learning about food. I asked the question, how do Americans know when they are really hungry? They are constantly being bom-barded by food stimulation. When they eat in restaurants people are constantly distracted by music, talk and visual stimulus; this way they are conditioned to forget what hunger really is." Communion was started to let people have a chance to learn how their bodies feel about food—how to pay full attention to food and to their eating.

Communion emphasizes "Take only as much as you need. There is a difference between want and need. Want is all ideas and need is real." People who eat regularly at Communion don't eat as much as when they first started coming in—even the members who work there eat less than they used to.

More than 70 percent of Communion's customers are regulars eating there four or more days a week. The total leftover food that comes back on the plates is less than a five-member family would leave, even with 160 meals a day. "Our customers realize that if they spoil food you have to cook more and they have to pay more."

They learned cooking by doing it, observing each time the quality of the ingredients, taste, cooking time and effects. They pay close at-tention to money as well as to the food consumed. A few months ago they noticed that the change box had less money in it than it should.

They put up a sign reading "Do we need a cashier?" The next week the money in the box matched the number of meals served and the sign came down.

Communion has been so successful that they were full for both lunch and dinner by the third month they were open. About every six months the crowd waiting outside got so large they just closed the restaurant and took an indefinite vacation for a month or so until people forgot about them and then they reopened. The restaurant served about 4,000 meals a month with expenses of rent, utilities and food at $1,500, so the remaining $2,000 to $2,500 was shared among the six workers who lived together and split the work so that only three were in the restaurant at any one time.

Since this article was written, Communion has changed hands twice, first being sold to a private person for $10,000, and later the ownership slowly evolved into the hands of another community group. Most of the unique elements slowly disappeared—talking is now permissible, there is music (either recorded, mostly jazz, or live), there are no second servings (just oversized first helpings), there is a cashier, etc. Business is not too hot, it is about half full at lunchtime. Quite a contrast to the joyful crowd when the idea was whole.

The Communion example emphasizes the fact that starting a business requires a series of decisions involving thousands of small elements. You can accept the traditional standards in making each of these decisions or consciously make changes. Our experience is that when making changes it is vital to think them through thoroughly because each one has an effect on the overall idea and operation.

A business with a very complete vision is McDonald's, which has a virtual monopoly on a way of doing business that no competitor seems to have caught on to. The underlying assumption is the fact that people love television and are virtually addicted to the feelings they experience while watching it. There are many people who, if it were possible, would never leave their television sets. Such viewers want to take that "television feeling" wherever they go. What McDonald's has done is translate that television feeling into an eating experience.

They have done this by using massive TV advertising that is totally tied to point-of-sale promotions that appear instantaneously in all of their outlets. At the same time you see McDonald's Fourth of July TV spot, with its red, white and blue symbols and a blue milkshake, the blue milkshake is available in your local McDonald's outlet. The same symbols that appeared in the commercial appear on the point-of-purchase materials and on banners hanging from the ceiling. You take that television experience from your home with you, and you eat it at McDonald's. (On the lighter side, you will have blue feces the next day from the dyes they put in their blue Fourth of July milkshake.)

The Green Gulch Greengrocer is a unique grocery store. The following account has been adapted from the original, which appeared in *The Briarpatch Book.*

The Green Gulch Greengrocer in San Francisco is an extraordinary business, although to outward appearances it has many similarities to other grocery stores. Visually the Green Gulch grocery doesn't look too different. It *is* cleaner than most groceries, much neater and less cluttered, even though it has less than 1,000 square feet of sales area. The *feeling* of the place is different. It feels warm, comfortable, truthful and inexpensive.

There are two reasons for the unique quality; one is the original motive, and two is the ongoing decision-making process.

The motive for opening the store was to serve the neighborhood around the Zen Center, which is the owner and operator of the grocery.

The neighborhood is more than 50 percent black people. Previously, the only store in the neighborhood was a small, high-priced one. It closed nearly a half year before the Zen Center decided to open one, and there were no interested renters for the store space. The community needed a store there as a focus; specifically the Zen Center felt there was a need for a low-cost grocer.

The grocery also fit the Zen Center's other activities. They had a farm on which they were raising vegetables and flowers as part of their practice, and there was a surplus of fresh, organic food. From the day the store opened, the decision-making process was very important. Every detail was carefully weighed, each decision was carefully considered in terms of service to the neighborhood, service in the form of a community focus and a low-priced store. One of the first decisions was to build a check-out counter in the middle of the store. This was done because Baker Roshi, the teacher-leader of the Zen community, wanted the employees to be physically close to the customers and to be part of the movement within the store, rather than to act as processors and guards standing at a check-out stand on the end of a dull production line at the exit. A counter in the middle does make the store less efficient than those with an ordinary check-out stand, but it enables the employees to chat with the customers, give advice and answer questions. As a customer, you feel a continual interaction with the people who work there and, of course, they feel much closer to their customers. The customers, in turn, seem to enjoy bagging their own groceries, which partially compensates for the inefficiency of the location of the check-out stand.

The store has many unusual little things about it that, taken together, have a great impact. For example, produce is marked with tags that are green, yellow or orange. Green means it is definitely organic, because they've grown it themselves or seen it grown with their own eyes; orange means it *isn't* organic at all; and yellow means it is in between, or "maybe." When we were there, Annie Styron, who wrote this article, asked David Chadwick, who was running the store, about some yellow-tagged potatoes; David stopped what he was doing and phoned the supplier and asked him if he personally "believed" that they were organic. The answer was yes, and David relayed that to Annie with his feeling that the supplier, himself, was a very honest person. Another example: the store buys from many more than the usual number of suppliers. This takes more time, but they want to deal with small suppliers as much as possible and they want to shop around enough to find the occasional low-priced deals on good products, like papayas with poor skins that were excellent inside and were sold to customers for as little as $0.12 a piece.

Still another example is the way the "spoilage" problem in produce is handled. Consistent with the Buddhist tradition of using everything fully, produce that has become discolored and too old to sell is put into a half-priced box, and the remains that aren't sold from that box are served in delicious casseroles to the students at the Zen Center. When fruit is involved, they juice it and sell it in returnable bottles. For all fruits and vegetables that are unusable, and for customers who want to contribute organic waste, there is a compost can that is carried back to their Green Gulch farm. All this is recycling, and the grocery store is immaculately clean.

This grocery differs from conventional health food stores and politically organized food co-ops because of its original reasons for opening and its ongoing decision-making processes. In health food stores it is rare to find so-called "junk food," and in politically organized co-ops it is rare to find food bought from giant wholesalers. In the Green Gulch Greengrocer you will find both. So-called "junk food" such as saltine crackers is available because the people in the neighborhood would have to walk many extra blocks to buy it, at real inconvenience. There isn't much "junk food," but several common items are carried. Similarly, when food from giant wholesalers is the cheapest, it is carried.

This carries over to pricing as well. Most of the prices in the store are multiples of $0.05 rather than $0.09, which is common ($0.39, or three for $0.99). They do this because there is no desire to mislead or confuse the customer, and $0.05 and $0.10 are much easier for the customer to add than $0.99. Of course, this makes it easier for the checkers to combine some totals in their heads at the check-out stand, too.

After the first eight months in business, the store was grossing $21,000 per month and hiring neighborhood kids to help out. The store's income finally stabilized at $33,000 per month, which is good for that amount of square feet. They now sell bakery goods from the Zen Center's bakery, which opened about a year later.

There are two problems with incorporating complete ideas into a business. The first is that frequently there are several people involved in decision making, and their combined ideas are not necessarily as powerful as an individual vision. Don't accept a group vision on the assumption that you need other people's help. A strong vision, to be alive, should be born whole.

Second, great ideas are very easily diluted by accepting conventional solutions. The Communion Restaurant could have bought tables that ignored the whole issue of shape, and they would have lost part of their wholeness. Any business will make compromises in the rush of meeting their opening date, but a real effort should be made to question each decision as strongly as possible.

The discussion in this chapter about keeping an idea whole may be mistaken by business school graduates as a euphemism for "marketing."

In conventional marketing classes, one is given examples of cases where a corporate symbol is used on every piece of stationery and every pen a company gives out for employee use. That kind of example is not what we are talking about when we say "keep an idea whole."

An instance of a conventional marketing campaign is the one Avis used a few years ago, "We Try Harder; We're #2." All employees had #2 buttons to wear.

As part of this Avis campaign, the president of the company deduced that a hard-driving company trying to please customers should be very flexible internally and that all departments should work together closely. He concluded, along these lines, that it would be a good idea for him to be able to phone any employee directly for information, to speed things up and not have to go through the chain of command. Occasionally, he pretended to be a customer and did the same thing. In a book he later wrote about this experiment he says the direct phoning created more problems than benefits. Unfortunately, he didn't think the idea through thoroughly and failed to recognize the need to let the process go the other way, giving the employees the power to call him directly.

A. P. Giannini, founder of the Bank of America, used the idea of accessibility brilliantly. He constantly visited the branches and offices of his bank, talking to the lowest-level employees on a personal basis, and always closing the conversation with the sincere offer, "Call me or come and visit me if there is something you feel is important." That is part of the complete idea in a company that *really* tries harder.

When you have something new, our experience indicates that it isn't worthwhile to mush over the difference between the old and the new. If the idea is really new, its newness must be confronted and dealt with openly. Here are two examples of businesses that disregarded this advice, one a bank and the other a coffee shop.

When Michael was at the Bank of California, the bank took over a large regional bank with a dozen offices, called the American National, which the local residents were quite fond of. To keep the takeover from appearing to be one in which a giant gobbles up an underdog, the Bank of California tried to make the changeover appear to be very gradual. They changed the signs to read: American National Division of Bank of California. They slowly modified everything visible to the public, while in fact the personnel and banking policies changed immediately after the acquisition.

Surveys of public opinion that Michael conducted about a year after the acquisition showed three public groupings: those who really knew what had happened and considered the marketing to be phony; those who were totally confused and were consequently avoiding the bank; and those who knew nothing about the changeover. The survey didn't find *any* people who said, "Oh, our lovely old community bank is just being modernized by its association with a big statewide bank," which was what the Bank of California management had hoped would be the result of the gradual changeover strategy. Five years later, most members of the bank management considered the transition a disaster. A completely honest and straightforward announcement to the public would have been more effective.

There is a little coffee shop and bakery near us called Taste of Honey. They have never asked for advice, but if they did we would tell them they have an idea that is new, and that they are hiding it to their detriment. All of the pastries and cookies they sell are made without sugar; in most cases they use only a little honey. Their location is fairly good and the "no-sugar" idea is very popular in their area, as demonstrated by the many people who go out of their way to get ice cream made with honey instead of white sugar.

Unfortunately, Taste of Honey doesn't make an effective effort to emphasize its uniqueness. The only mention of it is a long, wordy sign with small print located about six feet behind the counter, which only a person with exceptional eyesight could possibly read. One of the things the store could do is hand out antisugar flyers with each serving explaining what they are doing.

The net effect of the failure to communicate their unique idea to their customers is demonstrated by the kind of comments we've heard from people having coffee or leaving the shop, "Their stuff tastes kinda weird." The customers don't know why, and business isn't doing too well.

Summary

When you are starting a business with a new idea, work the idea out entirely, examine all its ramifications and nuances, keep developing it until you are certain of its validity and then execute it completely. The integrity of the whole will show through and your vision will be constantly supported by your customers as well as your imitators.

Tom Conlon assembling a windpowered generator

8 · GO SLOW

Going slow is fundamental to business. In the business world it is impossible to have solid, positive information about the unexpressed desires of your customers. The slower you go in making changes, the more opportunity you will have for feedback and the less chance you will have to make errors.

It is comparable to being blindfolded; you move very slowly so that you have more chance to correct errors and so that errors need not be irreparable. There are two especially important times to go slow in business: when you are getting started, and when business is going well.

Getting Started

Tom Conlon, of Aeropower, manufactured propeller blades for wind generators. The *Whole Earth Catalog* said he made the very best ones around.

Tom, a mechanical wizard in his early twenties, wanted to start a business producing generators to go with his propellers. He was technically qualified and had tradeskill, but his business experience was minimal. He didn't know how to raise capital and didn't seem to have any likely sources.

After analyzing his propeller business we were able to recommend that the good response from classified ads in *Mother Earth News* could be used to increase his sales volume and generate a surplus to be used for the generator business. His propeller business could support another employee if gross revenues went from $600 a month to $1,000. (Tom lived on very little, and always attracted loyal people who would work for very little.) We encouraged Tom to run regular ads in *Mother Earth News*, and suggested that when the propeller business was large enough he could hire an assistant. In this way, he could reduce his own work load and use the spare time to begin working on the prototype generators.

It was a slow process, but within six months Tom had an assistant. In the next six months he found enough time to make several proto-types and the related equipment to build more. Going slowly worked in helping Tom get a new business started. His patience and attention to the propeller company provided the capital for the generator business.

Fran's Simple City Systems store, which we've described before, sells products specifically designed for people who live in apartments and for people who move a lot. She has a good idea and spends considerable energy and time finding suitable products. Fran started work on the accumulation of inventory and on design of the store in October, with a store lease set to begin in December. This was not enough time for her to open properly. She decided to take the loss of revenue from not being open in December, January and February, and to have an official opening in March, when she had everything together. With a good solid publicity campaign, her opening was a smashing success.

The reader needs a caution about timing at this point. Sometimes Christmas, or other similar occasions, provide such an important dead-line that you must meet it. As a consequence, you must allow time to go slowly and still meet deadlines.

We advised a group of men starting a restaurant and bar business in some remodeled boxcars to open by the first week in December. At that time of year they could be instantly full. In their area, large numbers of people ate out the few weeks before Christmas and filled up all the available restaurants. The men met their deadline and have been full ever since. It was the first Victoria Station in San Francisco. They serve an excellent meal, with an open salad bar, in unique surroundings.

Henry came to us wanting to open a children's recycled toy store modeled on Toy Go Round. Henry wasn't nearly ready, though. When he came to see us, it was mid-October and he planned to open his store before Christmas. It was a new business for him and he had little prior experience. We knew that if he opened without an adequate inventory before Christmas, the business would be destroyed at its inception. Most likely he would be cleaned out of stock and inventory by the first people to come into the store. Those who came later would wonder what the store was all about and how it worked, but they wouldn't come back. Opening in time for Christmas, in this instance, would have destroyed the future of the business.

Why is going slow in opening a business so vital? First, because it allows time for you to observe valuable feedback, and second, because there is always more to do in business than anyone who hasn't done it before can conceive. It is not that things always get fouled up by strikes or floods, but rather that there are so many things that you never thought would have to be done.

When Fran first planned to open her store she figured it would take a few months to make the most important item, a specially designed loft. The special design turned out to be dependent on a type of wood that wouldn't be seasoned properly for a few more months, and urgent last minute scrounging for substitute wood was necessary.

In another example, Barbara wanted to hang paintings in the lobby of her gallery, but discovered that she would have to get theft insurance before many artists would be willing to exhibit their work in such a high-traffic location. Barbara then found that no one would insure her against theft until an alarm system was installed, which, in turn, was dependent on her getting a special telephone line. The result was a whole month's delay.

One of our favorite business examples is Simas Brothers gas stations, started in the early 1930s by a very wise man who had a good feel for the life of cut-rate independents. The business is now in the hands of his son Ted, with fourteen stations in the San Francisco Bay Area. Theirs is a vulnerable business: gas wars occur all the time as the giants deliberately try to put the independents out of business.

The Simas family has handled this beautifully. They have never borrowed money for anything, including real estate. Each new station was opened only when enough money had been saved to pay for it in full. The effect of this brilliant strategy is that there is no minimum, fixed overhead. When the giants cut the price of their gas to nearly the wholesale price, Simas Brothers can lay off their employees, stay in business at the lower rates, use up some of their "war chest" reserve funds kept just for this purpose, and not have any minimum payments that would drive them out of business. Going slowly in building the business was, for them, the only survival strategy.

Many times people have come to us anxious to do a big project, such as a feature-length film or an hour-long television documentary. Often their experience is limited to having been on a film crew or having made a six-minute, animated short in school. Enormous energy is required for someone with little experience to complete such grandiose projects, but there are always a few famous examples of people who succeeded by starting out big, and the beginners have heard of them. In presenting their case for a big film their logic is that "it takes a lot of energy to put together any film, whether it is twenty minutes or ninety minutes, so why not start out on the big one?" Our advice is always to start out in a step-by-step way. That way other people gain confidence in your ability, and each step upwards is a mastery of skills as well.

Jane believed in "the big film." She had an idea for a ninety-minute television documentary on an aspect of the woman's movement. She had prepared a beautiful $250,000 budget and prospectus, but her experience was limited to one ten-minute film and two television spot ads.

We suggested that she use some of her material to make a fifteen-minute program for a major TV channel that sometimes ran shows like hers. They usually used their own crews at a budget of $2,000 to $3,000, and could afford to pay her that amount for her material if they didn't have to shoot it themselves. Jane wasn't interested. She just repeated the logic about big and little being equally easy. Neither Jane nor her ninety-minute program have been heard of in four years.

On the other hand, Peter and his sister Nancy came to us when they wanted to do a film on gay people using a documentary-biographical style. Peter had done one excellent documentary that he had produced independently and that film, *The Holy Ghost People*, was in national distribution. We suggested that they borrow from friends using future earnings from *The Holy Ghost People* as collateral, and start working on the new film slowly with whatever money they had.

Peter and Nancy gradually built a loyal crew dedicated to the new film. They used the least expensive techniques available to make their film, including borrowing cameras and countless other items from their friends in the film community. As it turned out, people who were in the film and people who were part of the slow development were instrumental in the financing. The film, *Word Is Out*, is a huge success, was shown on the Public Broadcasting System network and has been made into a book.

From these examples the lesson is clear: when starting a business go slow in order to get a chance to generate a larger community for support, and to learn the vital lessons of your business fully and more clearly.

Going Too Fast in an Established Business

A typical example of going too fast was Darlene, a dance teacher, who changed her ad copy, the price of her classes and the paper in which she was advertising, all at the same time. She experienced a slight decrease in class attendance, but since she had made so many changes at once she had no way of knowing which ones worked for her and which worked against her.

A similar example was that of a harmonica teacher who sold cassette-tape lessons. A few years ago he changed the cover of his cassettes and some of the material inside and added a plastic bag to hang the tapes in the stores. Sales picked up a little, but who knows what caused it?

An even worse example was the too rapid changes made by Thousand Fingers, a collectively run crafts store located in a good retail shopping neighborhood. They reorganized their window, changed the positioning of their merchandise and moved the cash register, all in the month before Christmas. The slight increase in their revenue was not significant. Possibly some of the changes worked against each other. This all took place at a time when they were undergoing management problems. They only survived two months after that.

In all three cases, had the owners undertaken different parts of the changes slowly over time, they would have been much more able to evaluate the changes, and would have achieved measurably better business results.

When Business Is Doing Well

Paperback Traffic, which was located across the street from Thousand Fingers, changed one thing at a time and noted the effects. First they moved books away from the cash register and lowered the check-out platform. Increased business. Then they enlarged their magazine rack. Big increase in business. They changed the window and reorganized the book tables. No change. Finally some personnel changes were made that gave the manager time off. There was no change, which in itself was a good result because the manager was one of the principals and time off was a reward for him.

Businesses can make small decisions that can have irreversible effects. Don't meddle with things that work lest you make a major mistake.

The Bank of America made just such a mistake, which has haunted them now for twenty-five years. In 1952 there was a minor battle among the California banks on the issue of staying open on Saturdays. Bank of America held out the longest in the battle. While other banks succumbed to the pressures of the battle and closed their doors on that day, Bank of America stayed open, hoping to capture a bigger share of the market from people who wanted checks cashed on Saturday.

The problem was that many bank employees didn't like to work on Saturdays. Consequently, during the brief period that Bank of America was open on Saturdays while other banks were closed, a massive number of employees quit and went to work for other banks. Many of those who left were long-time career employees. These were replaced with inexperienced staff, new to the marketplace, who had a limited commitment to their work. The result was that the new employees made a very large number of errors which resulted in a bad reputation for the bank.

Even though the bank quickly ended the Saturday banking hours, the consequences were long-lived. In Calfornia the Bank of America still has a bad reputation among business customers for making errors, as a result of that period, in spite of the fact that their error rate is the same or lower than that of most banks.

Summary

Going slow is the most rational strategy for starting and running a business. It means paying close attention to your timing, planning openings and expansions so they reflect market needs and knowing that major changes will take longer to carry out than you expect. Most of all, in an ongoing business, it means making small, incremental changes that allow you to wait and see the effects of each change. The mistake of making many simultaneous changes means that the successful ones cannot be isolated. Such mistakes can be serious because small errors in judgment can have major consequences.

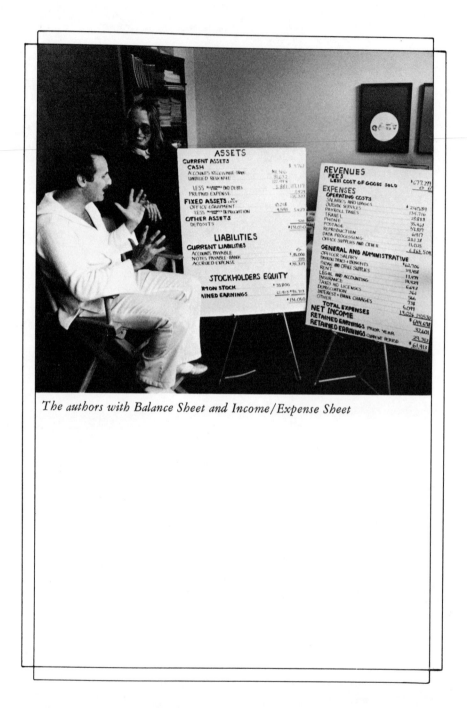

The authors with Balance Sheet and Income/Expense Sheet

9 · STUDY THE BOOKS

The "books" of a business are its financial records. Even the most rudimentary books can be surprisingly helpful.

The Granary was a small organic bakery/health-food store run by six women in the Monterey-Carmel area of California. When we first met to discuss problems they were having with their lease, we asked to see their books to get a better sense of their operation. They had no books. We offered to look at whatever records they did have, which included their checkbook register with a list of whom they wrote checks to, and another log book which showed how much cash they had received. Their log book recorded a day-by-day total of the money received with occasional marginal notes such as "Monday 23rd—$173.22 plus $15 I.O.U. from Jeanne."

From these records it was hard to offer advice, especially since we had never been inside their shop. We transcribed their daily sales figures into a weekly table for analysis and noticed, from one year's worth of sales data, that the business had a pattern of medium sales on Monday, a drop in sales on Tuesday, and rising sales each day thereafter, peaking on Saturday.

Since retail business sales usually rise steadily from Monday through Saturday, we asked repeatedly what was so unusual about Tuesdays? Was there something happening in the neighborhood or in their town? Did a railroad block traffic on that day? What were they doing differently?

After long and persistent questioning, one of the women remembered what it was they did differently on Tuesday; that was the day they cleaned the bathroom in the morning. A bakery sells its products to a large extent through their wonderful smells. The chlorine from the bathroom cleaning didn't mingle well with the natural smell of bread and rolls baking. It appeared to be hurting sales.

When we heard from them again they were cleaning the bathroom in the evening, the Tuesday drop in sales had disappeared and they were back on course.

What happened? Employees seldom notice consistent, recurring activities that can affect their business. Customers, however, can be affected because they are motivated by many subtle factors. Customers have great freedom to buy or not to buy; it is therefore important to have a sense of the subtle factors affecting their decisions. The vehicle and the tool for this is self-questioning. We become self-questioning by studying our books for clues. In the case of the Granary the books were the record of the invisible smells that were affecting business.

Financial records are a spectacular extension of our ordinary senses. They are to business what the telescope and microscope are to science, what the lab tests and stethoscope are to doctors, what radar and maps are to navigators.

What are the books?

We won't show you what they look like since they are a taboo in our culture. If we had examples of "books" in here, a lot of people flipping through would see those pages and put our book back on the shelf. People do the same thing with books that have pictures of naked bodies and genitals in them.

Most of us have been taught that "doing the books" is something for specialists like bookkeepers and accountants, just as hemorrhoids are the province of proctologists and vaginal infections are to be treated by gynecologists. Rasberry feels that until a woman has looked at her own genitals in a mirror she cannot claim her body as her own. Michael says that until you examine your books closely the business cannot be yours.

If you are ready to overcome the taboo of books, then read on; if not, then *do not go into business*! We have only met one or two people who ran their business well without keeping good books. Less than one out of a thousand people can run a business by the seat of their pants. What's the sense when business is hard enough? So many small businesses fail that trying to run one without books is like tightrope walking without a net while wearing cowboy boots.

When you look at your books, you are looking at a reflection of your creation—your child—and it is a beautiful, important barometer.

The simplest books are a checkbook register and a list of daily receipts. Those are THE BOOKS even for the most enormous corporation. The more accurate the checkbook register and receipt lists are, the more you can learn about your business. Most businesses we look at have only a little more than that.

The way the information in your books is organized is the whole skill of bookkeeping. How can you make your books more useful?

The checkbook becomes more useful when different payments are classified by some simple categories. Instead of looking through the list of checks and asking, "What is the $240 to Mastin Associates?" you can use a separate sheet of paper to create categories for expenditures such as rent, supplies, utilities, telephone, membership fees, printing and such. On this sheet you first list the check number, the amount and to whom paid, then separately list each amount under the appropriate category. Summarize these expenditures by totaling each column at the end of each month.

The same classification process applies to the record of sales. If sales are separated into descriptive categories in your receipt book, such as "Goods Sold Wholesale" and "Goods Sold Retail," or into major categories such as "Bakery Products," "Sales to Other Businesses," and "Coffee Shop Sales," you would have a clearer picture of your business.

Now you are an initiate and can brave the challenge of opening a book that has tables and numbers in it without shame.

There is a very logical and consistent path from what you now know to being good at keeping and understanding your books.

You may have some questions when you start keeping books, such as "How do I record an item that has been returned?" or "Where do I make a note that this check was to pay back a small loan from Jack, and isn't part of his wages?" As these cases come up, ask a bookkeeper or accountant for help. They can advise you about how the other initiates into this taboo subject have dealt with these questions over the past two hundred years. Their answers will consist of the proper, easy way to make a note, or to write in the number, so that later on you will understand the impact of that item on your whole business. Books are not cold; when you use them every day they become like comfortable, friendly slippers.

Where do our books lead us? They lead to a simple abstraction of the information we have collected called a financial statement. This abstraction is put on two sheets of paper, one called the Balance Sheet and the other called the Income/Expense Sheet. You can see what they look like in the background charts in the photo facing this chapter.

The Balance Sheet is a counting up of what we own and a comparison of that to what we owe. At the top are the things we own, starting with cash and ending with deposits that we have made to others. In the middle is what we owe, listed in the priority of who has the most legal right to be paid. At the bottom is the figure that represents the difference when the amount that is owed is subtracted from what is owned.

A Balance Sheet always reflects a specific point in time. At the top of the Balance Sheet it will say, very officiously, "December 31," or some such date. Whatever yours says, it is important to remember that this date reflects one moment in time. Usually Balance Sheet figures refer to the end of a month or year.

Why is this element so important to remember? Some businesses, or events within a business, are highly volatile. In banking, for instance, a bank can experience increases and decreases in their deposits of as much as 30 percent in one day. In such a volatile business situation, it is crucial to understand that the Balance Sheet reflects a moment in time, and that selecting another moment could give you figures that were different by 30 percent. The phrase used lightheartedly in banking to describe the practice of bringing a lot of money into the bank on the last day of the year is "window dressing." To customers, stockholders and regulating authorities, the matter can be more serious.

On a Balance Sheet, what you own and what you owe are listed in categories such as cash, inventory, property and bank loans. For each category there is an estimate of the amount of money (in cash, or in terms of the value of the goods or property) in that category. It is really an estimate in many cases because it involves assumptions such as the market value of objects if they were sold and possible losses if customers don't want to pay you. Since it includes many judgments and assumptions, each item and category should be questioned. What you own is shown on the Balance Sheet in dollar figures, but the new car you bought yesterday may have a resale value that is $2,000 lower today. The piece of land noted on your Balance Sheet at a worth of $15,000 might take two years to sell at that price.

The second sheet in a financial statement is the Income/Expense Sheet. It also deals with time but, rather than a moment in time, it deals with an interval of time. It will say at the top of the page, "June Statement," or "Second Quarter Statement," as it records the income and expenses of the business over that period of time—say from June 1 to June 30.

At the top of the statement is the income of your business. Reading down the page we find all the expenses of your business subtracted from that income figure. After all expenses are subtracted we find at the bottom of the page a figure that indicates net profit, surplus or net earnings. The last figure is the income less the expenses, and it is quite important to the business.

The main things to keep in mind about this Income/Expense Sheet are the following: What are the sources of income? Are they in cash? Do the expenses really include all the expenses involved in selling the items that generate the income? And do the expenses represent the real cost of the items involved?

Some businesses show only the cash received during the period being reported and others include credit. Under one system called "cash accounting," $6,000 worth of bread sold for cash in June would be reported. Under the other, called the "accrual system," that same $6,000 would be shown, but so would an additional $1,000 worth of bread that was sold in June but was not to be paid for until July. That means you should find out if the financial statement is a "cash" statement or an "accrual" one. Accrual is the preferred system among those who have learned to use it.

Expenses can also be ambiguous for the same reason. Under the cash-accounting system only the amount actually paid to the phone company is noted, while under the accrual system the entire amount owed will be recorded. The two figures can be quite different if you are several months behind in paying bills.

Similarly, there are figures omitted from the expense list. It is not uncommon for an owner of a business to work sixty hours a week, but not to show this labor cost on the Income/Expense Sheet because he or she lives on whatever money is left over on the bottom line. If the owner should ever get sick, or take a vacation, a real wage would have to be shown on the sheet.

Costs of materials can be equally deceptive. We remember a company that showed a very low price for the cost of the wool materials used, a figure that was much lower than the regular market price. It turned out that the wool was stray ends from a friend's carpet factory. This low price was a very precarious part of the business. If the friend was no longer available the final price of the product would have to be much higher.

The following illustrations show the relationship between the two sheets of the financial statement. In illustrations 1 and 2, you see two different sides of an object; can you picture what the object looks like

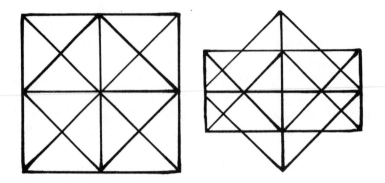

in three dimensions? These two images are like the Balance Sheet that shows the business at one moment in time, demonstrating the assets at that moment. The Income/Expense Sheet shows what went through the business over an interval of time. Neither one, alone, fully describes the business, yet considered together they become illustration 3, and give you a sense of the entire picture. When you compare financial statements over a period of time you get a much more solid feeling of what the business is about, as suggested by illustration 4.

What are the things we can learn about our businesses from studying the books? Two good things are: what days off you can take, and when you can take a vacation.

Sherry had bought Skin Zone, the small bath and scents business we've talked about, which she had previously managed for a period of six months. Now that she was the owner she had to work seven days a week to cover the costs of the loan she had gotten to buy the business. After a few months of working seven days a week she looked pretty bad and couldn't shake off her constant cold. With just a tiny amount of surplus cash, how could she afford to take even one day off?

We took a look at her daily sales record and found that Sunday sales were generally quite low, with most of the transactions in the mid-afternoon. Instead of keeping the store open seven hours on Sunday, Sherry decided to open it from 1:00 to 4:00 and hire a friend, who agreed to work for $3 an hour during those times. We knew from the books that even if she lost all of her Sunday business it would not significantly affect the net income.

The result: Sherry regained her health, which helped to improve the overall business climate, and the Sunday sales remained about the same. If Sherry had arbitrarily picked any other day it might have been disastrous. She was the business's best salesperson and shortening the hours on another day would probably have resulted in a net loss.

Keeping books is a very rational process. If you keep good track of reality by looking in your "mirror," you will discover what you need to know about your business. Books are like a computer, programmed by you to aid you in continuing your business.

Oz had a similar experience to Sherry's with his Roommate Referral Service. He wanted to take a vacation, but didn't see how he could without jeopardizing his business. Using figures developed from his own books he was able to find an ideal time period. From this data he could see that his was a very seasonal business, most busy at the beginning of the school year, and at the end of school when people moved away for the summer. He hired a helper during the most slack two-week period in March.

Another element to look at, on the income side of your books, is the different sources of income. Paperback Traffic Bookstore had reached a plateau in sales, although the neighborhood continued to grow in vitality. Jim, the manager, examined his books and found that magazines as a percentage of the total business had been slowly going down over the previous year, and made up only 20 percent of revenues. Magazines are often the first thing people purchase at a store that is new to them, so that the percentage should have been going up. Jim was encouraged to move the magazines to a more prominent location. The result was a dramatic increase in magazine sales and subsequently in book sales. In fact, the results were so energizing that the manager made a number of aesthetic improvements and total business continued to grow to the point where expansion was needed in less than a year.

Processes that are gradual, or are part of the structure of the business, often cannot be perceived intuitively by the operating personnel, as seen in the following example. This is an especially important reason why studying your books is so vital.

One business we worked with thought their income had been going upward for six years, even though their yearly sales totals varied erratically. When we looked at the income figures, what was really hidden by the erratic income was a serious situation. A few large service contracts were replacing many smaller ones at the same time that the staff and office space were growing. The combination was a mistake. In this case, as in many others, a few large clients can mean erratic income. When it comes in, it is in large chunks and the allure of the large chunks lead to lush staffs and lavish offices.

The variability of income to this particular business was covered by increased loans from the bank. The bank was impressed with the important new customer accounts and by how long the business had been operating. However, when several big clients went elsewhere the company was slow to respond by cutting costs, because they hadn't been carefully analyzing the information in their books. The company does not exist today. Moral: Let your financial statement tell you what is really happening in your business, even when it contradicts your own feelings and those of your banker.

An interesting experiment is to look at the financial statement of a small business without knowing the nature of that business, and try to guess what work they do. This is a very powerful exercise. For example, Michael recently looked at the Income/Expense Sheet of a small business for a one month period. The income was $9,000, and the cost of goods sold was over $6,000. The rent was $250, and the utility bill was $200. What was the business?

Michael was able to guess by asking a few questions. He found that the store was very small and sold retail. One would only find such a high volume of business being done in a tiny space, and with such a high cost of goods sold (the product is bought for $0.50 and sold for $0.75), if the product was food. The high utility bill suggested refrigerators, and his guess was an ice cream store. Right!

Try this yourself. Almost every financial statement is a give away for what type of business is being done. If you ask a knowledgeable financial person to guess the nature of your business from your statement, and they can't, you should be suspicious about whether your statement truly reflects the kind of information you want.

One of the most useful things a financial statement can show you is the cost per unit of your product. Often you hear people say, "This costs me more than what I am selling it for." They can come to that conclusion when they look at their unit cost.

In the case of the ice cream store, the $9,000 in income came from selling 12,000 ice cream cones at an average price of $0.75 per cone. The cost of each cone, based on the wholesale ice cream price, rent and everything else except wages, was $0.60. From this we can conclude that the $0.15 difference between $0.60 in cost and $0.75 in sales price has to pay the salary of the worker and the owner of the business. A $0.15 margin per cone for labor and management can be quickly evaluated. If we take labor costs at $3.00 per hour, that leaves three minutes to make each cone and give it to the customer. It doesn't take three minutes to make and serve a cone on the one hand, and on the other, customers are not in line waiting to be served every minute the store is open. If the ice cream store can't figure out a better ratio between cost and revenues, they will not be able to survive. This can be deduced from looking at their unit costs, something that most people understand at a gut level.

Whenever you visit a business you can make these same kinds of calculations. Start by seeing how many other people are shopping when you are there, and figure out roughly the amount of the average sale. Next, guess the cost of rent and the wholesale price of the goods. Then estimate the number of employees and try to figure out how much sales volume is needed to make the business work. See if you are right. If you calculate an overall loss for the business, check occasionally to see if it is still operating. If you figure that income far exceeds expenses, look for signs of expansion, the owner's ostentatiousness or employee unionization. Doing this exercise often over a long period of time will help develop your financial analysis abilities.

Frequently when giving business advice, we will make a rough estimate before talking to the owner or manager. With our imaginary financial statement in mind, it is a challenge to look at the real one and examine the differences.

Reading a business's financial statement is sometimes one of the most pleasurable aspects of consulting work. In some ways, it is like reading a private diary. It can reveal how much effort a person is putting into a business, what the personal priorities are, and often it will reveal small things about the person and the business that even he or she didn't see.

As an example, in looking at the books of a small do-it-yourself frame shop owned by Jeanne, a single woman, we noticed one man whose name appeared in the check register showed an increase in wages six months before our visit. One month before our visit, his name disappeared from the employee list while the amount of the owner's draw went up. We asked the owner about it, and she said, "I didn't intend to tell anyone yet but he became manager six months ago, and he just moved in with me last month. I think we might be getting married before long." Reading a financial statement can be very revealing.

Timeliness of financial material is very important. Think carefully about how fragile your business is, how quickly it could be destroyed if something you didn't know about got out of hand. With this understanding in mind determine how often you need to look at your financial data, and which figures are most vital.

A research firm we worked with employed sixty interviewers to interview the public over a five-hundred-mile radius. The firm accepted a fixed bid on a survey based on a questionnaire that they calculated could be completed in forty-five minutes. The cost of the survey was directly dependent on the interview time. Consequently, the questionnaire was tested to make sure it took only forty-five minutes.

After the testing was done, some questions were changed by the client, but no new testing was done. The interviewers who were out interviewing the public customarily did their work and billed the company at the end of the week. This particular research project was a rush job that was done on a Monday and Tuesday, and completed on Wednesday, with the bills submitted on Friday.

At company headquarters, the total wages owed to interviewers was computed by the bookkeeper on the following Monday and Tuesday, and left on the owner's desk to be approved Wednesday morning. The average interview turned out to be one hour and ten minutes in length, 60 percent longer than figured in the bidding. Since the facts were in a week too late, there was nothing that could be done. The company wiped out its previous two years worth of net earnings on this one job.

The company clearly erred by not retesting the questionnaire, but the lack of daily wage reports in a situation such as this, where a minor error could mean disaster, is the kind of problem that can be detected by having and using *timely* financial data. Wage reports should have been phoned in daily on such a large job.

This is not intended as a scare story. It is intended to strongly suggest that a thoughtful analysis of your business is necessary to determine how often you need to look at your financial information, and what information is most essential for your survival.

Summary

The books of your company are the most potent business tool available. Survival without good books is nearly impossible.

Your books consist of information taken from the check register and from a record of receipts. This information is arranged in a variety of ways to give you a picture of the processes going on in the business. It gives you a unique perspective on slow processes, as well as vital information on urgent aspects that can get out of control. Studying your books gives you a broad perspective on all the forces that act and interact to affect the health of your business.

Howard Sutherland

10 · OPEN BOOKS

No single element defines the distinction between an honest business and one that is not than the issue of open books. Somebody who is new to business and enthusiastic about it will usually bring out whatever pieces of paper pass for their books to show a curious visitor without hesitation. Yet 99 percent of the people in the general business world will have a reaction of total terror at the possibility of some outsider seeing their financial records.

Having open books means letting anyone look at your business records, especially your financial statements and the details necessary to understand them. "Anyone" includes employees, customers, suppliers and curious bystanders.

Many new businesses have open books. Glide Memorial United Methodist Church, where Michael works as the business manager, keeps the audited financial statement, including employment data by sex, skin color and ethnic origin, posted in front of its business office.

Emergency Services, a group of professionals in Washington, D.C. who help people in social action projects, keep their current financial statements on their office wall.

At the Yardley Frame Shop in western England you will find the books in a folder hanging by a string near the cash register.

Several hundred businesses that we deal with have open books. In many cases you may have to ask to see them, because there is no obvious place to put or post them. The fact of the matter is that so few people can meaningfully read books that the public seldom looks at the material. However, employees and friends do read them. The issue of openness and willingness of businesses to show their books does not depend on how many people look at them.

Why should a business have its books open?

There are several good reasons for open books that directly benefit the business. It feels good, and openness generates openness.

Howard's openness helped him raise money. He publishes the finest (and only) bicycle repair manual for the six thousand bicycle repair shops in the United States. Howard was ready to print his second edition and ran into several problems. The first was that he had borrowed to the limit of his personal credit to keep his business going, and the second was that the printer still had an outstanding bill from the first edition. Howard had presold some of the new editions at less than $12, and that was the break-even point by later calculations. What was he to do?

Howard considered taking advertising, which would have bailed him out of his credit problems at the expense of credibility among his readers. (Do you feel comfortable patronizing a Triple A motel when its so-called impartial rating appears on the same page as a paid ad?) What he did, instead, was announce his problem and then described honestly the state of his business to some bicycle product manufacturers at a trade show and asked their opinion about his taking ads. The universal feedback was "No ads!" After his announcement, two people came to him and offered to personally co-sign on a loan for him. Openness allows people to trust you and your motives, which are revealed explicitly in your books.

Openness works in dealing with debts as well. Dr. Jimmy had put on a big conference on nutrition that was a complete financial bust. He lost over $15,000, which made it impossible to pay the speakers and helpers at the conference. He didn't have the cash to pay the publishers whose books he had sold at the conference when their bills came due thirty days later.

We met with Jimmy about eight months after the debacle. His business was just getting going again as a result of offering small classes on nutrition. His concern was that after he had exhausted his resources trying to pay the conference debts as best he could, the people he still owed money to were hounding him. Dr. Jimmy had sent out several letters explaining his financial problems and still he was being dunned.

We looked at the sheets of paper that listed his creditors with the amounts owed to each and how much each had been paid. It was detailed and complete, and he had been very fair and persistent in his repayment. We suggested that he send a complete copy of these payment sheets to each of his creditors, which he did. Without exception they took the pressure off him. His open books were far more convincing than the standard letters he was sending out because the letters were typical of what creditors get all the time from deadbeats as well as from sincere debtors.

Open books can be very helpful in avoiding personnel problems. For ecological reasons, Cottonfield is a store that sells only cotton goods. It had been operating for six months when the three women who worked together in the store began to have difficulty with each other. The store required much of their time, and the two women who weren't owners wanted equity. The friction grew to the point where they had to confront the issues. The owner, Jane, an imaginative innovator in the fabric field, had brought the books up-to-date, and asked us to help explain them to the other two women. With the facts of the business clear it became possible to openly discuss wages, hours and future expectations in an atmosphere of mutual support. A more conventional business, with closed books, might have had to fire these loyal employees or might have resolved the problem temporarily only to leave problems to resurface later.

Open books work in many ways. One of our favorite illustrations of the effect of open books on the public concerns Communion Restaurant, discussed in Chapter 7. The money the customers put in the open till was being stolen. The restaurant put up a sign along with their financial statement, to remind people that they would have to hire a cashier and raise the prices if the thievery continued. Communion demonstrated to its customers that their behavior directly affected business and, in the process, renewed the evidence of their own honesty with this action.

The father of open books for us is Stewart Brand (although he gives the credit to Steve Baer) who created the *Whole Earth Catalogs* and printed the complete financial data in every issue. More recently Stewart has been publishing the *CoEvolution Quarterly*, in which he still prints the complete financial statement, with a number of wonderful consequences.

Stewart has an abundance of contributors who send in articles, book reviews and suggestions about new issues, because the readers feel they are a part of the community of the magazine. In addition, Stewart is regularly offered financial advice by readers, often unsolicited, and usually very good. Publishing his financial statement in each issue keeps Stewart very aware of the financial issues involved in the magazine. Interestingly, in the early days of *C.Q.*, when subscriber growth rate was low and several quarters looked very bleak, an unsolicited gift of $25,000 came in the mail. Did that ever happen to *Look* or *Life* magazines? The readers of those two magazines never even had a hint that the magazines were having financial trouble, even though the death throes lasted several years.

Not only do communities grow out of open books, as in the case of C.Q., but they also thrive on the openness, especially when help is needed. You recall the story of the boy who cried "Wolf, wolf," too many times and the townspeople finally stopped coming to help him when they found out he had lied. The converse of this story is particularly important. The more often you are open and honest, the more you can count on other people to come to your aid.

The Zen Center had a horrendous fire at their mountain monastery and the mountains and hills around it were all burned. The monastery used as a guest retreat in the summer was saved but the costs in saving it were high. Zen Center sent an extraordinary letter four pages long, with color photos of the fire, to all its direct community and to the previous guests of the mountain retreat. In the letter was a complete list of all the expenses incurred ranging from bulldozer charges to the cost of replacing the telephone lines. Their costs had come to over $60,000; the donations sent in, in response to the letter, totaled more than $150,000. The material was presented in the letter, not in a pleading, poor-mouth way, but in the straightforward manner the Zen Center always uses to discuss its costs and finances; it was a natural thing for them to do and it was accepted, as such, by the community.

What about Open Books and Trade Secrecy?

The Jorgenson brothers make a wonderful small brass pipe called Protopipe, that is commonly used for smoking dope. It is precisely machined, and good for the lifetime of an ordinary pot smoker. A while back, a fast-talking promoter came in and offered the brothers a lot of money to go big time with their product and to hype it with fancy marketing and cheaper production. The brothers said no. Then they wondered how they could legally protect their product from being copied by the promoter in spite of their objections. (They couldn't trust the courts of law to protect their product since it is used for purposes that most judges consider to be sinful.)

So the Jorgensons just let life unfold.

The fast-talking promoter had a small shop produce identical-looking copies of the pipe at a much lower price, and packaged the whole thing in a can with a fancy label. He called the pipe "Tomato." Soon Tomato was showing up in a lot of stores where Protopipe was sold. The lifespan of Tomato was about eight months; the stem of the pipe was not carefully machined, just soldered together, and very soon buyers found their pipes falling apart. Word spread rapidly that Tomato, with its big flashy packaging, was rotten, and stores stopped carrying it. Not surprisingly, appreciation for the fine manufacturing quality of Protopipes was increased.

Arnie has a company that makes a fine electronic pick-up for guitars and wind instruments, which is patented. His company is called FRAP, short for Flat Response Audio Pick-up. Arnie doesn't want a cheap duplicate of his product sold to an unsuspecting audience, and he's found an interesting way to use the trade secrecy laws to protect his little company without his having to be a paranoid ogre.

Arnie's assembly techniques are what he is trying to protect. This could be difficult since he has a number of people working under his supervision. His solution was to get copies of the trade secrecy laws, and some examples of court cases that established precedents for dealing with people who had violated these laws. He put all of this into readable English, on a few pages, that made the whole issue very clear.

When Arnie wanted to use an employee for the patent-related work, he would let the employee read the material, make sure the person understood it and ask if he or she wanted the job. If the answer was "yes" he had the employee sign a copy of the material and keep a personal copy.

There are no threats or hidden agendas here. Arnie feels comfortable and open, and no one has ever violated his secrecy.

What about Open Books and the IRS?

We have no respect for the IRS and nothing nice to say about it. Our reasons for strongly disliking that institution have nothing to do with the amount of taxes collected or with the methods used to collect them. We are offended by the moral cretinism that infests the IRS bureaucracy.

In the late 1960s and early 1970s, at a time when one of Michael's uncles was an undersecretary of the Treasury, a group operated in the basement of the IRS building. Called the SSS, or Special Services Section, the group was made up of loyal, long-time employees of the IRS, who were working with the FBI to pressure, harass and intimidate anti-

Vietnam war groups and the Black Panther party. A congressional committee exposed this years later.

Glide Memorial United Methodist Church, where both of us have worked, was very active in urban social change issues in those years and came under attack by the FBI, and later by the IRS. The result was an IRS examination that dragged on for nine years, cost the church over $50,000 in legal fees and gave us a chance to see the most disgusting underpinnings of our federal system of government.

The IRS, through its SSS group, succeeded in destroying hundreds of well-meaning organizations. For Huey Newton, the leader of the Panthers, they created an atmosphere of terror and pain that lasted for years.

The people responsible for these outrages have never been identified or punished. There is no redress of this kind of behavior of the IRS.

Even with those five vitriolic paragraphs about the IRS, we still say you should have open books and pay your taxes. Right from the begining.

It is very common in small businesses for the owners to take a percentage of the daily cash transactions, and not to report it on their income taxes. This is especially true in retail stores where sales are in cash. The percentage the owners take varies with the type of business; some bar owners take 25 percent off the top in cash, some small clothing stores take 10 percent, while a bakery might take 5 percent of their sales without reporting it.

The question in these situations is, "How do I have open books if someone is going to tell the IRS on me for taking unreported income?" The answer is simple. Be honest and report all your income. Get the best tax advice you can, pay the least tax you can, argue, lobby and protest the tax, but be honest.

Another common situation is one in which the owners of the business have never reported anything about the business to the IRS. In most of these cases, the owners were not making a lot of taxable income, choosing to keep the business off the income tax rolls because of the paper work, and because it is a way to avoid withholding taxes, which come to an average of 25 percent of their employees' wages. By not paying withholding taxes they are able to pay their employees better salaries.

Usually the facts of the situation are pretty straightforward. The business is growing, has little income and this type of arrangement helps create a small niche in which the business can survive and operate.

Take as an example a carpet cleaning service that is just getting started by offering very low prices. As the business grows, pressures may converge on the owners to force the carpet cleaning service to finally go legitimate and start withholding employee taxes. The word "finally" is important. Finally can be two years after starting the business, or seven years. The problem in the meantime is that there is usually a great deal of anxiety for the owners, especially if the consequences of this non-reporting are understood. The real decision in this kind of situation isn't *whether* to pay the withholding taxes or not, it is *when* to start paying them. (See "Withholding Taxes," in Chapter 15.)

Our experience in these cases has been that the paranoia and anxiety are not worth the money saved. The solution is to confront the real issues, head on, and decide when you are going to start withholding. Really. Losing sleep, hiding money, getting secret savings accounts across town, asking people to make checks out to different names just isn't worth the effort for most "otherwise honest" people we know.

If you are convinced your business can't survive with withholding, then form a partnership among the employees. With this approach, which is described in Chapter 15, you have every employee file his or her own business tax forms. In that way, everyone takes responsibility for doing their own reporting and withholding.

Summary

Having open books is one of the most powerful ways to get useful feedback from your community. It will bring you help when you need it most from genuine supporters who sympathize with your motives. It helps build and maintain true customer loyalty. It provides the groundwork for employee participation and loyalty. Above all it is the clearest indication of an honest business.

There are many people who want to have open books, but have fears about it. The usual fears we hear cited for not having open books are competitors and the IRS. "Competitors" are not even discussed in this chapter, as such, because an honest business doesn't have competitors. The operating advantages of better service to customers, community support and lower prices so far outweigh the conventional way of doing business that having open books is never a disadvantage.

On the other hand, fears of the IRS are realistic and worth examining. As an institution the IRS constantly enforces the moral values of the society and, occasionally, the moral values of perverted bureaucrats hidden in its basements, or the perverted President we elect. It is an undesirable institution, but unrelated to the issue of open books.

To survive the onslaught of the mammoth agency, keep accurate records and pay your business taxes. If you are not witholding your employees' taxes in your business when you should be, we suggest that your resulting anxiety is probably not worth it. Partnership is the solution we suggest. In the long run, you'll find that the emotional benefits of openness are worth finding a way to achieve it.

Customers in the Dartington Cider Press Shop, Devon,England

11 · COMMUNITY

A community is a group of people who have common interests and needs and share a common activity. All businesses are communities. The people who are involved with *The New Yorker* magazine are a community. The readers share a common set of reading interests that reflect a similarity of values. The magazine staff works to provide the literary and design qualities that the readers want, and to harmonize these with the desires of the advertisers and distributors. Together, the readers, advertisers, distributors and staff form *The New Yorker* community.

The advertisers offer a specific range of products that the editorial staff believes are appropriate to the general values of *The New Yorker*'s community. The magazine goes to great lengths to exclude products and content that it thinks are inappropriate to the community. For example, when *The New Yorker* says it won't take ads from Frederick's of Hollywood (for sexy female lingerie) it is speaking for its community, which includes advertisers, readers, distributors and employees.

Books, too, have a community. The second book by an author usually lists the first book and often the cover has some version of the phrase, "Another book you'll enjoy by . . ." Who is the "you" in that sentence? It is the community that shared the common experience of reading the first book.

It is clear that a barber has a community, a bank has a community and doctors and grocery stores do, as well. Even giant corporations have communities. When they are big enough, everyone in the nation is their community. The telephone company, AT&T, has to deal with all of us at just about every level of their business. In their employment policies, their investments, research and new services, they must continually deal with the American public. Early in the century, Theodore Vail was chairman of AT&T, and he understood that his company's future role was tied to the community. This understanding greatly contributed to his reputation as a great businessperson.

The concept of community as described here is significantly different from the traditional business view of "the market."

The marketing view emphasizes the similarity of attributes shared by buyers and potential buyers, as expressed in such statements as "The market for macadamia nuts is all people 25 to 50 who have incomes over $20,000." The way to sell nuts to this market is to give them away free on airplanes.

The community concept is much broader since it includes everyone involved in the process of planting, harvesting, processing, packaging, financing and distributing macadamia nuts. Using community as the reference, macadamia nut sales would be promoted by extending the personal contacts of the people in the existing community, and supporting their friendship networks with samples and seasonal gifts. The promotional giveaway would go to friends of nut company employees, not to airline passengers.

All businesses are communities. When a business is open and honest, the community can take pride in its activities and the business can enjoy a wide array of benefits that any community offers. The specific benefits include useful advice from the community, many unique sources of financing, new customers and superior employees.

Peter Murray started and runs the Dartington Cider Press Shop, in the Devon area of England, which sells chesses, ciders and jams made by families in the surrounding countryside. The products are all labeled with the store's name in large letters, and the producer's name in smaller letters. All the people whose products are sold in the store actively solicit customers and encourage other people to become new suppliers. The store is thriving as a wonderful community affair. Members of the store's community encouraged Peter to take their products to fairs in northern France, where they were well received. The store's community has also provided a steady supply of their friends and relatives as enthusiastic employees.

Finnegan's Wake is a prosperous bar, located in a feminist and vegetarian neighborhood. From its inception the partners decided to split one third of their annual profits with their customers and staff. The first dividend was paid out in the form of two expensive, electrostatic air filters so that smokers could smoke in the bar without bothering the non-smokers. The second dividend was a big party with free drinks and a lavish banquet offered for three hours one Saturday afternoon. This party became a tradition, and was carried on for many years. The results for the bar have been spectacular. It is continually full nearly year round, and the atmosphere is always friendly and upbeat.

One of the owners, Tom Hargadon, wrote us about the business: "I was part owner of Finnegan's Wake. Each January and July we had community parties to celebrate being there, with the regulars of the bar, friends and people who heard about it. We had food, beer and wine, and a fine time. The party in July was called the Birthday Party since it was around the birthdays of most of the partners.

"What I was attempting to set up with this bar was a place where dialogue could happen. These days given the problems with the word 'dialogue,' I often say a place where real talk happens. What is required is an ambience that people sense that tells them, 'This is a place you can be as open as you wish with the others here. You will be approached to talk and you can approach others. You can choose to talk or not talk and you won't get hassled, especially in a sexual way.' Sexual pickups at bars are a repertoire of verbal games and are not really talking.

"It took us eight months to find a place in the neighborhood we chose with a liquor license, four months to negotiate a lease, three months to get approval from the Alcoholic Beverage Commission, and two months to renovate. Simultaneously, it took us five months to get a Small Business Administration participation loan of $28,000.

"The capital cost was $70,000, with $42,000 from the nine partners. The liquor license cost $45,000. We were all friends; I had been an original partner at the Plough and the Stars in Cambridge, Massachusetts.

"The arrangement with the partners was that everyone working in the bar would be paid the same amount, $5 per hour. Money paid for management would be at the same rate, and kept to a minimum. After all bills were paid, investors would receive 15 percent return on their money out of the first profits. Then we would split additional profits among the staff, community parties and organizations, and additional managerial salaries.

"The crucial, early decisions included having an open, airy place where people could see in, come in for coffee and fresh orange juice as well as booze, and pricing the drinks slightly higher than the other bars in the neighborhood did, so that people would think about coming in, and have a reason for doing so, not just for a quick drink.

"From the first day, the employees were able to earn $5 per hour, and the bar broke even for the first six months. We got the atmosphere we wanted, open and talkative. From there on we started making money.

"For the first three years, revenue increased about $100 per week, per month. Before I sold my share of the partnership, we were giving the partners $15,000 to $18,000 every six months, the staff got bonuses of $8,000 to $10,000, and the disbursements to the community ranged from $3,000 to $3,500 per month, including the semiannual parties. This has gone to community groups in the area for childcare, political organizing and all kinds of activities.

"So far the talking is going well, the bar is a community institution, and the staff and investors are happy."

The number of cases in which a traditionally defined community participates directly in a business is great. Each of us knows of businesses in which the husband, wife and a cousin work together. We also know of cases in which a group of friends got together to start a business. Community in this traditional meaning makes sense in business.

This community awareness is especially important for new immigrants who must start out in an environment where they are unknown and are often not trusted. The behavior of these newcomers is different, and frequently feared. The immigrant community provides the new businesses with guidance, financing, employees, information and everything else that a business requires. All businesses have the same needs, yet we seldom see the elements as clearly as we do when we consider community in the narrow sense of immigrants or families.

There are many ways to benefit from the community of a business. When a business is about to make a change in direction, is having difficulties or needs new impetus, that is the time to solicit help from the community. Several examples come to mind.

The *Briarpatch Review* staff had put out six issues of the quarterly magazine and were burned out. Everyone who was known to be interested in the *Review* who lived in the geographic area, including previous writers, collaborators and artists, was invited to a dinner where the problems were aired. New staff volunteered and promptly began working with the old staff on the next issue. The transition was complete in a few months.

Dick Raymond and Sam Yanes sent out a promotional flyer for a new publication to potential subscribers, people who had had good experiences with an earlier publication with which Dick had been involved. They were able to raise enough money in the return mail to finance *Big Rock Candy Mountain*, a journal of innovative school experiences. (Under current postal regulations such solicitations are not allowed.)

Diane Sward Rappaport obtained ads for her music magazine, *Music Works*, from her old friends in the music business. She had been a promoter for many years and was completely trusted in her community. The revenues she got from phoning around for advance ad sales were enough to pay for work on the first issue.

There are problems in dealing with friends, relatives and others who are close to you when loans are involved. Special care should be taken in these cases. Our experience with such arrangements is that they are most successful when people put the business arrangements between friends and relatives in writing *and* include in the written agreements a discussion of all unspoken expectations, along with a formula for resolving disputes should they arise.

For example, one of the members of a printing partnership went to his father to co-sign a loan so the partnership could buy a major machine for their business. Father and son wrote an agreement separate from the co-signed loan. The agreement included the provisions that the father would not interfere in the business in any way or even offer advice, and that if the loan were not fully repaid on time, the son would take a full-time job and work for three years to repay the loan as best he could. After that time, the issue was to be forgotten and the slate cleared. In addition, no cousins should expect to be hired by the printing partnership unless it were unanimously agreed upon.

We've seen a number of other agreements between parents and their offspring in business, as well as between cousins or siblings. There are often provisions for more participation and advice by the lender, and there are different contingencies for the settlement. In one case, the parents were to be shipped the entire inventory of the business for them to liquidate if the loan wasn't paid off in time.

Similar written agreements are vital between friends as well, and need great explicitness about emotional consequences should payments be late or circumstances change. A wonderful book that deals with this issue is *The Living Together Kit*, by Shara and Warner, which gives sample contracts for many personal situations that are similar to business loans. (The book is produced by a business team who publish as Nolo Press, 950 Parker Street, Oakland, CA 94710, $8.95.)

Summary

Community is the environment in which business exists. Community includes suppliers, employees, customers, advertisers, friends and relatives. The process of looking at a business from the point of view of evaluating its role with all these support groups is a powerful one. If your business is open and honest, your community becomes the most important asset of the business. You can look to your community for advice, financing and new customers and employees.

When you deal financially with relatives and close friends, extra concern is needed. These people play such a vital, long-term role in your life that you need to make sure that agreements and contracts are explicit, in writing and fully understood.

Carole Rae in her studio

12 · PAYING BILLS PROMPTLY

It may be obvious that other subjects covered in this book—capital, book-keeping and management—are really relevant to running a small business. "Paying bills promptly" is a subject that is not covered in any other books about business. It is considered so fundamental or so trivial that it hasn't seemed appropriate for others to write about.

This book is based on experience rather than theory, however, and we have been confronted time and time again with the reality that the way a business pays its bills is quite important.

The way a business pays its bills is seldom an activity that is visible to employees, customers or the rest of the world. However, it is extremely important to some of the recipients to whom it is quite visible. To them, it is as important as a handshake in the sense that a handshake is often used as a measurement of a person's character. Payment practices are only one element on a credit report about your business, but this single item can have a subtle influence on your entire business reputation.

An easy way to understand the importance of paying bills promptly is to look at it from the recipients' point of view. Arnie and Vivi ran FRAP, a small electronics manufacturing business selling electronic pick-ups for musical instruments that was discussed earlier. We asked them to show us a list of their customers with the percentage of business that came from the four largest ones. They didn't have this information so we asked them to make up a list of all the stores to which they had sold their products in the past three years, and the size of their orders.

Arnie was the electronic wizard of FRAP, and handled production. Vivi was in charge of sales, bookkeeping and "business," so she compiled a list of their customers. The customers were scattered all over the U.S. and Canada, with no visible geographic concentration. We asked them both to sit down and go over the list, even though Arnie was usually in the back room soldering while Vivi handled the business end of things. When they were asked about each customer they both quickly responded with useful information.

"That's Jake, he's up in Toronto, orders three or four units at a time and pays cash."

"That's Sound Exodus in L.A. John there always tells us at trade fairs that he wants ten units, and then orders one and takes three months to pay for it."

"G. & E. Sales is on 42nd Street. They display our stuff well and usually pay when they reorder."

We didn't ask about paying practices but both Arnie and Vivi considered those details a key part of the business description of their customers. Between the two of them they gave us details on 125 customers without checking any files.

FRAP was a hang-loose operation at the time and we were very surprised at how much they knew about each customer, and especially the precision of their knowledge about bill-paying habits. But it's not really surprising; their business depended on this kind of knowledge for its own survival.

If you are the business paying the bills you can expect that kind of attention to your payment practices from people who do business with you. In many instances, your payments may play a vital role in their day-to-day survival.

Paying promptly has some tangible benefits.

The Briarpatch Auto Co-op was one of the first "long-hair" businesses in Palo Alto when they opened in the early 1970s, and they received no support from most of the local businesses. The co-op manager, Bill Duncan, worked very hard and was careful to pay all the bills promptly. Within six months, nearly every supply house in the area was helping them out with advice, discounts and quick service. It is vital for an auto repair shop to be able to call a supply house and ask about a '64 Dodge truck differential and be told that some other part in stock will work just as well, and to know where tires are being sold below cost in a closeout sale. It is important to have suppliers tell you about new products and tools that work, and those that don't work. Bill earned the respect of other businesses by paying promptly, which more than made up for the amount of hair on his head.

Often suppliers will extend credit to you during hard times if you have had a good relationship with them in the past. This is particularly true if you are candid and let them know your situation fully.

Nan Hohenstein, who is a brilliant publicist, handled public relations for Simple City Systems. In the first months before and during her opening, Fran always paid Nan's P.R. fees in advance, as required. Money became tight when Fran was reordering a lot of merchandise and she realized that she would not be able to pay her publicist for a while. She discussed her situation with Nan, who agreed to spread the payments over a three-month period. In effect, Nan was loaning Fran money, a loan that grew out of an earlier trust and was possible because Nan had a positive cash flow at the time.

A small silkscreen company called Sisisote, that specialized in African designs, was having financial difficulty. The owners talked to their creditors about the need for longer payment schedules and explained how dependent their business was on a few supply sources. One of the suppliers helped them apply for a loan at the supplier's own bank, and gave them an extra sixty days to pay their bill.

Paying bills promptly is sometimes crucial in a small-business community because of the many interconnected parts of the support systems.

An example of these linkages was visible on Tuesday afternoon in Carole Rae's weaving studio where four women were working. Joan rents space from Carole for her spinning business and, on that Tuesday, paid her monthly rent. Carole, in turn, paid wages to Jennifer, her bookkeeper and a part-time weaver. Jennifer took part of her wages and walked across the room to pay Joan for some yarn that she had bought from her the previous week. That wasn't the end. Joan then paid Margaret for some spinning she had done for her. Margaret took part of her spinning wages and paid them to Carole for her part of the rent for a house they shared. The same cash went through many hands in a few hours; the community of support was visible to the four women that afternoon.

Summary

A small business needs to pay its bills promptly. This practice is important to keep our own communities functioning smoothly. It is important to a business, when it runs into financial problems, to have the respect and support of the businesses that supply it. Paying promptly indicates our understanding of each business's role in the chain of interdependency that affects all business.

13 · MANAGEMENT

The whole theme of honest business as developed within the framework of this book leads to several unusual conclusions about management.

Management in an honest business plays a role much the way it does in any other business, but the specific elements of open books and sharing with the community mean that the issues of management have to include feedback from all sorts of people who wouldn't ordinarily affect management decisions. When suppliers read your financial statements, your mother works for you part time and a customer volunteers her services in the office, there are new issues management has to confront.

What is management, how do you get it, why should we have it and what is unique about management in an honest business?

Management can be thought of as the system of communication among people. Suppose four people are bird watching. In its most rudimentary form management would be the quiet words passed among the group signaling that a red-tail hawk is coming in low from the northwest, and the certain knowledge that if one person scares away the bird he or she will be severely reprimanded by the others. Management includes wearing appropriate clothes so as to be inconspicuous to birds, having a good atlas to refer to and using a book to log birds identified. Management supplies channels for dealing with the information, the quiet voices, the expected reprimand, the use of tools; it is not the information about the hawk. At its most rudimentary no one notices that this system of communication among people is management; at its most sophisticated level in the governance of hundreds of millions of people, it involves large staffs applying constant attention to communication. We are concerned with the specific systems of communication that have evolved for business.

Business management is a set of ideas about communication practices. Ideas we associate with the term management change with different historical periods and are different in many cultures. In our time and culture, the set of ideas that we call management is widely taught as a set of skills in universities, in community college evening courses, in the military service, in weekend seminars and in work environments. These skills can't be picked up through reading alone and we recommend enrolling in one of many institutions established to teach the form of management prevalent in American culture. These courses have titles such as Personnel Administration; Supervising People; Management by Objective; Financial Management; and Corporate Policy and Practice. If you are interested in some supplemental reading we recommend three out of the hundred books published. (See page 120.) They describe the concepts, philosophies and terminology of management.

There are a number of management practices that have evolved in our culture which are very powerful. In production, for example, the techniques of PERT Charting (it has many other names) is in use to plan the flow of supplies, sub assemblies and major components into a final product that is continually coming off the production line. A PERT Chart identifies trouble spots and time lags that can be critical. This is a powerful tool with a wide range of refinements; however, even at its simplest level, it is useful for a small business that engages in construction, manufacturing or assembling. If your business is involved in any form of assembly or manufacturing, the management skills associated with production control, quality control and purchasing will be invaluable.

In personnel management, the most powerful tools are the personnel file and the periodic review. For a business with five employees, it consists of five files. Each file has in it the wage payment records, preemployment application and related data, and the full written records of each personnel review. The "periodic review" of personnel is the record of a face-to-face conversation between each supervisor and supervisee. Each person in the conversation describes their own perceptions of the job conditions for the previous period and discusses plans for the coming period. A synopsis is written down. For example:

> *Supervisor*: Your attention to details has improved significantly in the past six months, the number of returned letters and similar errors has dropped by 50 percent. I have been told by the people around you

that they feel you are more helpful to them but you still have a pattern of leaving your work messy, as we talked about last Friday.

Supervisee: I have found more support from the people I work with but I need more accurate instructions from you about your mailing needs and my suggestions for sorting the mail have still not been tried out.

Plans and expectations for the coming period are discussed and recorded. In an honest business these files are open to everyone and anyone can add their own comments, preferably signed. The periodic intervals between reviews should be scheduled seasonally and for maximum value should be kept completely separate from interviews dealing with pay and wages.

The following is a sampling of the best arguments for the need and role of management in a small business given by Peter F. Drucker, in *Management* (N.Y.: Harper & Row, 1974):

> Not so long ago it was widely believed that the small business needed little or no attention to management. Management was then thought to be for the "big boys." One still hears people in a small business saying, "Management? That's for General Electric; we are small and simple enough to do without attention to management." But this is delusion. The small business needs organized and systematic management even more than the big business. It does not need, to be sure, large central staffs. It does not need elaborate procedures and techniques in many areas. In fact, it can afford neither large staffs nor elaborate procedures. But it does need management of a high order. . . .
>
> The small business has limited resources, above all, of good men [sic]. Concentration is therefore essential to it. And unless the key activities are clearly identified and assigned as responsibilities, there will be diffusion of resources rather than concentration. [Key activities include finance, personnel, dealings with the outside called marketing, production, and the associated technology and quality control.]
>
> The need is for a little thought, a little organization, and a simple reporting and control system—no more than a checklist, perhaps—to make sure that the work is actually being done.

Even in a business with three people, these responsibilities need to be assigned and regularly reviewed. Finance includes the responsibility for bookkeeping, budgeting and planning the cash needs of the business. Personnel includes the record keeping needs discussed above and all of the personnel considerations about health care, vacations, child care, etc. Marketing includes all of the needs for dealing with customers, suppliers, friends, and seeing that time is available for substantial community involvement and that community needs are effectively heard and considered in the business. It also includes visiting customers' homes and businesses to see how your product or service is used.

Management requires the assignment of these responsibilities and reports that evaluate effectiveness, regardless of how small the number of people involved.

As Peter Drucker says, "[A] small business needs very few figures. And most of the figures it needs are easy to obtain, especially as precision is rarely needed. But the figures the small business needs the most to be managed are not, as a rule, figures the ordinary accounting model provides. They are figures which relate the present condition of the company and the present deployment of its key resources to anticipated future developments, both to identify opportunities and to ward off danger.

"The small business cannot afford 'big management,' if by that is meant an abundance of staff, of procedures, and of figures. But it needs first-rate management. It needs to structure the top-management job precisely because it cannot afford an elaborate top-management structure."

An interesting management system that we looked at was used by the Church of Scientology and modeled on U.S. Navy concepts. The church had seven management components: finance, personnel, communication, production, marketing, quality control and education. The quality control component resembled the Inspector General's role in the military, and had responsibility for finding staff complaints and dealing with them. The church is very evangelical and establishes offices in many hundreds of cities. The interesting thing is that when a new person or married couple is sent out to establish a new branch office all seven components are immediately established and, as new people join up, the responsibilities are gradually divided up. That means that when two people open a new office each will have a portfolio of responsibilities: one person might have three and the other four. The seven management components are imbedded in the church's office procedure even when there is only one person with no one else to manage.

What is different about management in honest business? The openness of the business is in itself a central structural element of management. It means that the honest business has a built-in number of extra channels of information to deal with, ranging from suppliers' views to the views of relatives and employees. These extra channels provide better customer information and business wisdom that might otherwise be lacking.

The most unique thing about honest business management is that it has what contemporary management theory is struggling to develop for business: structural openness. The business that starts with its first owner/ worker assuming openness *as a premise for doing business*, will develop to maturity with a key *structural component* of management that other, traditional businesses can only strive to imitate. Building openness into the structure of the business is different from introducing it as a technique for participation when the business is already mature.

The example of the Bolivar experiment described later on in this chapter (see pages 116–18) shows the power of openness when introduced to a traditionally operating business. The examples of the businesses created by four men (Giannini, Vail, Procter and Penney, on pages 175–82) also indicate the power of openness in cases where the founding managers had personnel operating practices based on their individual honest practices.

For your business, the effect of openness in management will be very particular. It is the component that makes the business specially different.

It takes great personal determination to overcome the traditional business community pressures for secrecy and to persist in openness. It takes a fresh mind to constantly, daily, examine each decision to determine whether it fosters openness or leads to secrecy.

We cannot tell you the immediate, first day effects of openness. Many examples of businesses based on openness have been given in this book; their innovativeness is a reflection of their structural commitment to openness.

Management is a set of skills that is badly needed in every size business, and training in these skills is widely available in the United States. When contemporary management as it is practiced in our culture is combined with the structural commitment to openness, the result is innovative business forms, extra channels of valuable information and more effective management. The combined effects of contemporary management and structurally integrated openness are too new to give a broad range of concrete directions, but several suggestions from our experience are worth considering. The first three concern management personnel—the use of outsiders on the Board of Directors, the effective use of an outside counselor for promoting team cooperation, and the need for vacations. The second two concern general practices that recognize the needs of employees.

Outside Perspective on the Board

Earlier chapters have included many examples of the value of outside opinions and advice on business decisions. Allowing a variety of opinions and advisors to play a role at every stage of decision making effectively broadens the range of experience brought to bear. The willingness of owners or managers to expose themselves to this variety of experience is an a priori recognition of the best way to deal with business decisions.

Institutionalizing this access of outsiders to your business decisions is a good management decision. Open books, employee participation in management, capital from friends and family are all methods of institutionalizing this process. Another example is Point Foundation's Elijah Chair, which can be used wherever a group of people meets regularly to make decisions.

Michael was on the six-man Board of Directors of Point Foundation. Point was created to distribute to the public in the form of grants $1.25 million earned by *The Last Whole Earth Catalog*. The Point bylaws called for seven board members, but at the outset one member quit. The other members were too new to each other to agree on a new seventh member so the board invented the concept of the Elijah Chair. They decided the seventh member of the board would be different at each meeting, thereby providing a degree of freshness and self-awareness that the six board members knew they would quickly lose over the years as they worked together and became "old cronies."

Initially, the board allowed the seventh member to have all the power enjoyed by the rest in making grants. The first Elijah promptly made a grant to his wife—an act specifically prohibited the other board members by law. The Point board promptly realized that power to give grants without the responsibility for their consequences wouldn't work. From that point on the role of Elijah was ex-officio, limited to advising, interacting and disputing, and restricted from making legal commitments. Each successive Elijah played a powerful role in shaping the direction of grant decisions and in bringing vitality to the board meetings. Similar roles for outsiders exist in many business situations where teams, committees and task forces work together on a regular basis.

Outside Advisory on Management Cooperation

When the San Andreas Health Council, one of the first groups committed to providing a holistic health center in their community, found themselves in difficulty, they asked Richie Gordon for help. Richie had been a financial and spiritual advisor to many small businesses and collectives in the Bay Area. In addition to being a financial wiz, Richie is a student of psychosynthesis, an approach to integrating the personal, materially oriented aspect of the person with the transpersonal, mystical self.

San Andreas provided extraordinary classes and health practitioners to their community, but was desperately understaffed, and had no funds to hire more workers or to hire a fund-raiser. From their perspective, all the problems they were experiencing stemmed from the lack of resources and energy, so what little time they had was focused on trying to raise money. They were caught in a hopeless downward spiral.

From Richie's point of view there was real potential for the health council to succeed. San Andreas had a pleasant building at a convenient location, a network of interested, committed people, and they were providing a valuable service to their community.

This newly formed group needed a process to integrate the needs of a small business with the possibilities and potentials of a holistic approach to health. It was crucial, at this stage in their development, that the qualities of wisdom, healing, compassion, humor and understanding that they valued in their practice be expressed in all aspects of their organization.

In dealing with the health council Richie applied psychosynthesis to the organization as a whole by treating the business as if it were a being with a "self," a living being with purpose and qualities seeking expression. A central core was formed comprised of staff, the most active practitioners, teachers, board members and concerned community people. This group of eight to twelve people met each week for the next eight months.

Richie believed San Andreas would succeed to the degree that they could be true to the purpose of their organization. If the group could embody and express its unique purpose and qualities, it would solve the energy and money problems.

As facilitator at the weekly meetings, Richie related all discussions back to the purpose and "self" of San Andreas, which created a growing sense of mutual connection. The possibility of a working organizational structure developing around their group was stimulating and exciting. People gained confidence and clarity and resources began to flow.

These weekly meetings were not confrontational and did not focus on personality conflicts. People were encouraged to be supportive of one another's work and to seek ways to meet their needs as a group. Several exercises were used to aid the movement toward group integration.

It was important that each group member could experience being the central administrator of San Andreas, could feel the pressure of the myriad of needs constantly clamoring for attention. One person would sit in the center of the group while the others formed a circle around him or her. Each person in the circle picked a different need of the organization to champion, and simultaneously began to plead, cajole, lecture, request, yell at the center person to respond to *their* need. "Marketing needs a bigger budget," said one. "Finance needs another person," yelled another. When the person in the center could stand no more, they stopped the process. Out of this experience came an increased appreciation of the demands made on the administrators, as well as an agreement on the ranking of the priorities of the organization.

Group members were led through a guided fantasy enabling them to imagine that they were the core of San Andreas, the entity that is the organization. They all closed their eyes and allowed symbols representing the four most basic needs of San Andreas to emerge in their mind. They had a dialogue about these needs and then were instructed to imagine these images were climbing a mountain. They observed the needs fighting and the needs cooperating. When the needs reached the top of the mountain, a bright sun shone warmly upon them. Within the sun was the face of a very wise person who could answer any questions or uncertainties they had. Each member of the group spoke with the wise person about their needs and priorities, and what actions to take. This powerful exercise revealed that nearly all the members of the group had the same experience. Clarifying and expressing the "spirit" of San Andreas was everyone's most important need and would provide the key to dealing with the business problems of the organization. "Spirit" was the image of their healing service to others.

At the end of eight months of meetings the objectives of the health council were being met. A greater number of volunteers had come to work at San Andreas, responsibilities were being shared by a larger group of people and revenues were up. Programs expanded and more members of the larger community were participating. The core group became self-sustaining and Richie Gordon phased himself on to another project.

Getting Yourself Outside the Business

The issue of vacation is surprisingly important in the management of a small business. The prevailing view in industry is that vacations are a reward for good labor and a necessary respite from the work situation. Many people who run small businesses hesitate to take time off, not because of lack of money or fear of problems arising in their absence, but because business is their passion, their love, and they would rather spend time working than doing anything else.

There are two strong reasons why small-business owners and managers need vacations. First, it is important for them to be far enough away from the business to be detached from old patterns and ways of thinking. This will allow them to more readily see world trends that shape their business and will expose them to different views of reality, which in turn bring fresh insights into their business practices. Changing the environment from time to time is a specific tool to help deal with the forces affecting business.

The second reason for a manager to vacation is to give others in the business a chance to assume responsibility. The absence of the manager shakes things up, tests other people's strengths, shifts the portfolios of responsibility and lets subordinates go it on their own.

One result is that employees often learn what management responsibilities are and see that they don't want to be full-time managers. Another is that they see what the manager's work is, come to understand it and therefore are able to play a more constructive role in the future. Sometimes when a manager is vacationing, new ideas are tried that work. Often minor problems that were not visible under management supervision come to the surface during the vacation, problems that then can be dealt with when the manager returns. The surfacing is preferable to letting the problems smolder unnoticed, only to explode later. Occasionally a manager returns to find that the staff didn't get along too well during the absence and that structural and personnel changes are necessary to make the business work better.

Supervision of Employees

In addition to the general questions of management structure and practices we have discussed, there is the specific issue of the supervision of employees.

As you hire more people in the business, the issues of supervision become more acute. Even with openness built into the structure of the business there are established norms of behavior in our culture that influence the needs and perceptions of the people who are being supervised. Their input into the communication system is taken for granted here, but the founder or manager's ability to hear what is said is not taken for granted. There are two areas of difficulty: one is how to deal with the people who jointly participated in the creation of a business; the other is dealing with hired personnel.

Starting a Business with Other People

Often people starting their own businesses have charismatic qualities that attract others to help them. Assuming they have the tradeskill that carries them through the creation stage, a common development is that the person who started the business overlooks the expectations of the helpers while thriving on their energy and support. The usual consequence is that many of the expectations of the helpers who become employees are not met. This results in serious problems within the organization.

Two problems common to such businesses are high turnover of valuable personnel and litigation concerning business ownership rights. The way to avoid these troubles is to encourage written statements at the outset from each person involved in the new venture. These statements should emphasize the helpers' expectations on the following points:

1. What do I get if the business does very well, in terms of wages, ownership, responsibility and recognition?
2. What happens if we fail and loans are outstanding?
3. What if my talents don't really fit in after things get going? How am I to be compensated for my time and effort?

These questions must be dealt with before the business gets going, and discussions on each point should be resolved in clear agreements.

The common excuses to avoid dealing with these employees' expectation usually are: "We don't want to dampen everyone's spirit and enthusiasm," or "We are good, wonderful people who trust one another completely."

It is almost a rule of business that people will cooperate as long as their mutual needs and interests coincide. Good management involves getting these needs out in the open and dealing with them directly.

In relationships with employees there is a spectrum of supervisory styles, ranging from authoritarian order-giving to complete participation with consensus. It is common to find wonderful, honest people who operate very close to the authoritarian end of the spectrum but think they are conducting a participatory organization because they are so loving with their staff. This is really what was once called paternalism, which we now term parentalism.

Parentalism is a bad management practice. One of our friends who ran a business was a wonderful, motherly woman who went out of her way to personally help every one of her employees. She would bring chicken soup to the homes of ailing employees, give lovely parties for each employee's birthday and meet staff members at the airport when they returned from vacations. Warm and motherly as she was, she only let one other staff member help her deal with the financial problems and complexities of the business. As a result, a time came when it *appeared* to the employees that business was doing very well and they weren't getting appropriate raises. When the owner said she couldn't afford to give them more money, they didn't believe her and went on strike.

As the financial facts of the business slowly became visible it turned out that so much business had been lost during the two months before the strike that half of the employees could not possibly be rehired. In addition, the owner was so shocked by her "children's" ingratitude that she lost all heart for the business and closed it down within a year.

In our experience, employees should not be sheltered from the problems of the business, even in an authoritarian structure, but rather should fully understand the worst problems as well as the joyful successes. Most important, in such situations employees should be encouraged to participate in the decision-making process. Employee participation in management decisions is not the same as employees *making* management decisions. There is a spectrum of participation ranging from employees giving advice to complete employee control. Openness is required for effectiveness throughout this spectrum.

How effective a founder/manager is in dealing with employees is related to his or her ability to understand employee attitudes. With most employees the motivation for working has a great deal more to do with security than it has for the person who starts a business. Founder/managers are often surprised when employees choose a pension plan instead of profit sharing, or a salary over piecework, or a defined job with a known promotion schedule, over one with free-floating responsibility and possible large rewards. Many of the contemporary ideas of management that involve increased job responsibility are unappealing to workers who prefer job security. The following material on the Bolivar Experiment makes this point.

Innovative Management: The Bolivar Experiment

In the interest of increased productivity, we commonly find men and women treated as replaceable cogs in the machinery of industry. They have little personal satisfaction and no sense of security from their work. The highly competitive auto parts industry is notorious for dissatisfaction among its workers and is a prototype of the problems facing U.S. industry.

In the southwest corner of rural Tennessee, in the automobile mirror plant of Harmon Industries, an important experiment has been taking place since 1972. Sidney Harmon, chief executive of Harmon; Irving Bluestone, vice-president of the United Auto Workers; and Dr. Michael Macoby, author of *Gamesmanship* and head of the Harvard Project (and a friend of ours), joined together on a project to improve the lives of the workers involved at the Harmon assembly line. They wanted to create a work situation that would be economically viable and personally satisfying. The Bolivar Project, named after the Harmon mirror plant in Bolivar, Tennessee, became the first U.S. project developed jointly by management and a labor union for the purpose of stimulating "human development."

The aim was not to increase productivity, but to make work more rewarding. The challenge was difficult at the Harmon plant in Bolivar because it was in a rural, rather than an industrial, location and many employees had to work at menial jobs in order to maintain the farm life they preferred. There was also a long history of management-labor disputes.

Innovative management experiments traditionally have resulted in lowering labor costs by eliminating jobs once productivity increased. For this reason, there was a lot of justifiable resistance and initial suspicion toward the project on the part of the Bolivar workers and the union. This resistance and lack of trust had been anticipated by Harmon, Bluestone and Macoby, who drew up a written contract or "shelter agreement" guaranteeing workers that any gains from a speed-up in production would be equitably shared with the workers. This written guarantee, built into the union contract, assured that changes made by employees during the experiment could not be eliminated at the whim of management.

At the start, a Working Committee was formed consisting of five management people, five union members, Michael Macoby, and his staff. (Michael, incidentally, is a disciple and co-worker of Erich Fromm's.) They met, not as the adversaries of the past, but cooperatively, to deal with problems of heat, cold, ventilation and safety hazards that plagued the workers. The project spread from 1972 to 1975 with similar core groups formed in each department, ensuring participation from the shop floor.

What was learned from the experiment that is useful for the small, honest businessperson? Several results so far are meaningful. In 1975, Harmon Industries was in danger of losing a major contract and, with it, one hundred jobs at the Bolivar plant. Management opened its books and, together with the union, reexamined all the factors in order to come in with the lowest bid. Management found ways to operate on a lower than usual margin of profit, and in combination with higher production they were able to save the contract. The bid was accepted and the jobs were saved.

The Working Committee found a wide range in the workers' level of interest in participating in decisions. Some wanted to keep their outside lives separate and their minds uncluttered, while others gave more time and attention to the job. An independent evaluator of the project, Dr. Barry Macy, says that since the workers are left alone and not bothered, they have become self-motivated. The workers decide when to start or stop a project. Because of this new freedom from direct supervision productivity has increased significantly. He says, "Within the group there is a strong sense of teamwork. One member of the group indicated that this in itself gives his job more meaning and is the reason he no longer comes to the plant feeling, 'I can't face it.'"

According to Michael Macoby, "Increasingly, deliberations of the Working Committee consider how new programs will affect different people. If those who are quicker get to leave early, what happens to those who are slower? Will they be pushed to work beyond a safe and healthy pace? Democratic decision making becomes a process of evaluating alternatives according to human criteria, rather than a clash of selfish interests.

"Many employees have also benefited from educational programs. The first classes were initiated because participants in experimental programs who had increased their productivity had extra time. While some individuals wanted to go home early or to earn more money, others asked for courses in subjects related or unrelated to work. In the spirit of the program, anyone can be both teacher and learner. Employees both offer and request courses in subjects ranging from welding and sewing to piano playing and literature. It is significant that courses were instituted in public speaking and writing. Some workers have realized that both effective participation and leadership require confidence gained by skill in communication. Although courses are advertised only in the plant, all are open to anyone—Harmon employees, family and members of the community."

Openness in Management

Louie Durham was the manager of Glide Foundation, an endowed Methodist church that was very active in the social change movement in the late 1960s. Louie worked with a team of four other ministers and their staffs. His style of management was very open and participatory. At one point, Louie was confronted with pressure from his board of directors and several staff members to write a policy on several sticky personnel problems. Louie began examining the whole issue of "written policy" and decided that it was not open enough for his style of management. Policy is too hard to change and too inflexible in its interpretation once a board has voted on it. He chose the alternative of a set of written guidelines for new employees that listed prior actions that the staff had taken on these issues as examples, and emphasized in the guidelines that each future case had to be examined individually on its merits. The result has been a very flexible management style, with a minimum of written policy, that still remains twelve years later. Listing prior examples, without deducing a rigid policy, was an unusual and imaginative consequence of choosing openness.

Management of a Collective

On one end of the spectrum of supervisory styles is the collective with concensus decision making. Although the terminology is recent in American business and the concept seems frightening to many traditional managers, concensus decision making is the norm in Japanese business and is currently being tested and adapted to our culture. Good Times

Graphics is a collective of eight people that has been operating for more than a decade, and which grossed more than $300,000 last year. New Games is another collective of ten people, that is over five years old, with over $600,000 in annual revenues from their training programs. Fort Help is a health clinic with over twenty-five working members that has done well for more than a decade. All three are true collectives which we know personally that have thrived. In a concensus supervisory environment the structures of operations and responsibility closely parallel traditional businesses—there are bookkeepers, office managers, salespeople, etc.—but the decision-making process is different. Often you will find that managerial responsibility is rotated as are jobs entailing drudgery.

In the successful collective, the issues of administration are separated from the issues of decision making. Individuals are selected from the collective to administer the decisions and report back to the decision-making body. In a typical example the collective of workers at a retail clothing and notions store decided to keep accurate books and inventory records, and to minimize the number of salespeople working. A task manager was agreed on to carry out these decisions, a person was selected to be responsible for the books and records and two floor supervisors were chosen for different shifts with the responsibility of keeping the number of salespeople to a minimum.

It took three months before the processes set in motion were carried out. Each of the people with responsibility for a task reported back to the collective, of which they were also a part, and got help, guidance and support. When a person with a task responsibility reported trouble in getting cooperation from another, the issue was discussed openly by the whole collective. A manager's responsibility was not to fire or threaten people but to remind fellow workers of the group decisions, of the general direction of implementation, and to make minor on-the-spot decisions that supported the overall tasks and then to report progress to the decision-making group.

Collective processes are considerably slower than top-down traditional decision processes, but the results are much more effective and are much more satisfying for the participants. In a traditional structure, decision making is authoritarian and parallels the administrative structure. The "boss" makes boss-level decisions. Frequently, such decisions are not executed and, even worse, it is common to hear of decisions that are sabotaged by lower-level workers who were not consulted. In a well-run collective the decision making is slow but effective.

Summary

Management is the system of communication that people use to work together. Each culture has its own styles of communication and organization. Within our culture there are several functional categories that each business needs to recognize: marketing, quality control, finance, personnel. Most of these administrative skills are taught in schools and are especially worthwhile for anyone in business. Honest businesses, with their open practices, have special advantages in management because communication is more effective, clarity has a higher value and wisdom and promptness are more likely. There are added problems because more channels of communication are kept open and more time is expended. Openness does not lead to any specific generalized management techniques but each individual business, as it incorporates openness in its day-to-day decisions, is led farther down a path of creative solutions and personal satisfaction. Outside advisors in the business are encouraged, as is broad-based decision making; parentalism is discouraged.

For further reading on management, we recommend the following books:

Drucker, Peter. *Managing for Results.* New York: Harper & Row, 1964.

Koontz, Harold. *Principles of Management.* New York: McGraw-Hill, 1972.

Strong, Earl P. *The Management of Business.* New York: Harper & Row, 1965.

Gary Warne as a frog at Circus of the Soul

14 · FUN

Business should be fun. Without fun people are left wearing emotional raincoats most of their working lives. Building fun into business is vital; it brings life into our daily being. Fun is a powerful motive for most of our activities and should be a direct part of our livelihood. We should not relegate it to something we buy after work with money we earn.

There is very little tradition in business about fun. The common association of fun in business is the visit from a salesperson who notoriously brings a regular supply of jokes along with the merchandise.

Our close friends Bahauddin Alpine and Sherman Chickering have built fun into their business, *Common Ground Directory*, their quarterly, forty-page publication that lists individuals, businesses and institutions that offer growth, spiritual and healing services. The businesses that are listed pay $20 to $40 for the basic listing in the paper, in hopes of getting customers, clients or students for their classes. This paper has been copied in Chicago, Minneapolis, Los Angeles and several other areas with Bahauddin's encouragement.

The success of the publication depends on effective, wide-scale distribution of the quarterly; in the San Francisco Bay Area, 50,000 copies are distributed. Bahauddin and Sherman found that the best distribution system is to have all advertisers take their share of papers and distribute them in places near their businesses and in other places they frequent. To help the advertisers do this, *Common Ground* throws a party the night the papers arrive from the printer and invites all the advertisers to pick up their share of the papers. These gatherings are such fun that few people would miss them. There are also side benefits to this process, one being that advertisers, in talking to each other, are sometimes able to improve their ads. Another is that they get to know what is happening among their peers.

Gary Warne ran a used paperback bookstore (Circus of the Soul— mentioned earlier). He loves books, and it was the right business for him. He built fun into his work in many ways. The most noticeable was his offer to customers: "A free book if you wear a costume into the store." It made business a surprise for Gary and for the customers. The store became a unique place in the neighborhood.

Gary told us some other short stories about the Circus: "Another sign on the door said, 'WARNING: Every book in this store has been rejected by its previous owner as either irrelevant or boring,' and if customers thought a price was too high, I had a battery-operated fighter plane that hung from the ceiling. I started it up and, as it flew around the room they had three chances to hit it with a dart gun. A hit won them half off my price.

"I remember one guy who wanted to go for double or nothing (no one EVER hit the plane in two and a half years). He lost and paid twice what he would have for *Madame Bovary*. I also had a window sign that offered 'half-off sale on paperbacks.' Inside was a box of paperbacks cut in half."

Oz's roommate referral service shared a space with Gary when they were both getting started. People looking for a place came to Oz's and paid $6 to look through his listings of apartments and houses to find roommates. The people doing the listing were not charged. This rapidly became a boring business for Oz because the people searching for a new home were usually in a state of emotional turmoil associated with the anxiety of moving, and they took life very seriously. They would come in, pay their $6, and hastily sit down to intently pore through the files.

In response Oz became a practical joker. He bought exploding firecrackers that went off when he closed his desk drawer, got a device that made loud sounds when his chair moved, installed a toy airplane that buzzed across the ceiling and arranged for a rubber chicken to fall, unexpectedly, from the ceiling, making a wild noise. Oz found that people who couldn't respond joyfully to this bizarre world didn't make very good roommates. On "Circus Day" Oz also offered free roommate referral service if people wore one of the costumes from Gary's collection while they were looking through listings. The surprising thing was that, even to save the $6, many people would NOT put on a costume! To be fair to the customer Oz also had a rule: no fee if the customer made him laugh. We loved to visit Oz's storefront business.

Nearly every business situation can provide a way to bring fun into the lives of employees and customers, yet the hardest thing to overcome is the awesome prevailing taboo against it.

The *CoEvolution Quarterly* has maintained a tradition of having fun since the days of the *Whole Earth Catalog* ten years ago. Every noon there is a volleyball game. Visitors participate, other neighborhood groups join in and people often bring their friends along for the luncheon game.

Carole brings constant fun into her weaving studio by renting space to a wide variety of interesting people. At various times she has had in her studio a one-man band who practiced there, spinners, stained-glass makers, dyers, graphic artists and a juggler. The constant flow of unusual people and their friends creates a fun-filled environment.

Bess Bair, the tap dance teacher, takes her best students out to perform, free, on the streets of San Francisco. They are known in the streets as Rosie Radiator and the Push Rods. When you become a good enough student to be chosen as a Push Rod, you get a chance to perform with the group at free shows around the city. It is good for Bess's business and fun for all.

Jim has a factory store in Santa Rosa, California, that manufacturers portable massage tables. Every Monday afternoon, he has a masseuse come in to do his back and the back of any employee that wants it. A unique employee benefit.

If these examples don't stimulate ideas in your mind because the businesses seem too bizarre, or because business and fun seem antithetical, examine some of your own feelings and resistances. If you find yourself in a business that is no longer satisfying, no amount of clowning around and no number of interesting people passing through your office is going to change that. Having fun in business is not meant to mask dissatisfaction but to enhance your enjoyment of life. Going out of business should always be an option.

There is room for fun in every business and circumstance, even in giant corporations. For example, one of our favorite managers at the Bank of America in Sacramento had what he called "Mickey Mouse Day." On that day the staff would close the branch at exactly five minutes after three and go off for a party. Of course the books didn't get closed that day, and not all deposits were processed; but those were all promptly handled the next morning. The fun of Mickey Mouse Day was that no one ever knew when it was going to happen. The employees knew it when they arrived in the morning and saw a Mickey Mouse doll on the manager's desk. The doll seemed to appear whenever it was most needed.

Finally, fun can be introduced by modifying an existing business. In Aspen, Colorado, there is a restaurant-bar in the main mall called the Sidewalk Cafe. The new manager, Kim, introduced a simple plan. All waiters, waitresses and bartenders are encouraged to come in an hour before their shifts begin and cook a dish. Their dishes are listed on the daily special as long as they last: "Gene's Bacon Quiche," or "Ann's Red Hot Chili." The customers and the staff love it.

Summary

The opportunities for fun in business are endless. They are the natural consequence of running an honest business. Fun is a spontaneous part of any business when the owners and managers love what they are doing and the books are open. Fun is natural where friends and relatives participate, and where the business understands its role in the community it serves.

Send us your experiences. Let us know when the first business fails because the people in it are having too much fun.

15 · SHORT BITS OF ADVICE

Accounting, Accountants

"I'd love to find a warm, friendly accountant who listens to my problems, gives good advice about the business, takes the time to explain things to me, and knows all the shrewd angles about avoiding taxes." A lot of people are looking for this mythical being. Forget it. If such an accountant exists, he or she lives in a small town in Idaho, and has no intention of leaving. What most of us settle for are accountants who do their job well. For these, you'll have to ask around for references because a lot of accountants are sloppy, don't care about their clients and give poor or irrelevant advice. If you acknowledge that the best you can do is to get one who does a competent job, then finding that one attribute is a worthwhile accomplishment.

The role of an accountant in your business can range from the simplest advisory one to the most complete accounting service. When you are starting out, you may want an accountant to look at your books and help set them up, so that you understand them well enough to do them yourself. Later you may have a bookkeeper who prepares the monthly records, and will use the accountant to prepare quarterly statements, year-end figures and to do the taxes. At some point the business may be large enough to require an audit or accountant's statement for a bank loan or a public report. In the case of a non-profit business, an accountant's statement or audit may be required by donors and regulatory agencies.

As with lawyers, people tend to treat accountants as authority figures.

Remember, your accountant is paid by you, and it is your responsibility to be knowledgeable about what he or she can or cannot do for you.

The best accounting book for people beginning a business is *Smalltime Operator*, by Bernard Kammaroff,* and a fair manual for teaching you how to read financial statements, especially those of corporations, is *How to Keep Score in Business*, by Robert Follett.†

Advertising (see also Publicity)

If you want people to know what business you're in, the first step is by word of mouth, followed, at fifty paces, by publicity and, at another twenty-five paces, by paid advertising. Word of mouth means people telling their friends about your business. Publicity means descriptions and mentions of your business in public media. You don't control the content of these descriptions. Advertising includes all the promotional events and items in which you control the description of your business. Advertising is a suspect method for tooting your own horn, and is often mistrusted by potential customers. Advertising has come to be considered synonymous with manipulation and, in that sense, has no place in an honest business. The concept of advertising in this book refers to useful information such as special sales and new merchandise, not to teasing, alluring or persuading hype.

The most important reason to treat advertising with caution, and to absolutely avoid using it as a first choice of communication, is that it can be HARMFUL. When people find an out-of-the-way product or store that is not advertised, they proudly tell their friends about it. If it is advertised, then these same people are *far* less likely to tell their friends. People trust recommendations from their friends, and their stamp of approval is the best method for building your business.

People are so distrustful of advertising that the word "honest" is not even usable in our era. When Michael was a banker, he developed a service that made checking charges very easy for the customer to understand. He wanted to call it an "honest service charge" system since all the rest of the bank charge systems were designed to confuse and cheat people. The marketing director for the bank, Bob Person, pointed out that the only businesses to use the term "honest" in advertisements were used-car dealers and credit jewelers.

* Bell Springs Publishing, Laytonville, CA 95454, $6.95.
† Follett Publishing Co., Chicago, IL 60600, $7.95.

If you decide to advertise, try to keep a wide range of advertising vehicles in mind. Most people assume that advertising should be done in newspapers, or on radio and TV, but in fact many other approaches can be more effective.

When developing an advertising strategy, begin with the most obvious tactic. For a storefront business, the first step would be one with local impact, such as distributing sale coupons door-to-door in your neighborhood, and posting information about your store on community bulletin boards. For a business offering a specialized product or service, the most closely available market might be reached through a professional or trade journal.

If your business depends on an accessible location, begin with signs in, on and around your building. Consider sandwich signs in front of your store, with benches under the trees. Keep that kind of service in mind. Murals that are approved, and perhaps even done by neighbors on the outside walls of your building, are also powerful.

There is an interesting business, Thumbtack Bugle, run by Richard French, that posts notices for other businesses in all the laundries, coffee shops and public notice boards in our area for $50.

The objective when advertising a storefront business is to make useful connections in people's minds between your product or service, your store and its location. Landscaping and murals can do that as effectively as can countless other approaches. One woodcarver in Santa Cruz has crafted the doors and signs for nearly all the businesses in his neighborhood. When you are in that neighborhood, you overwhelmingly associate his style of woodcarving with the local businesses. That area is now associated with his craft. In another small town, the ceramic ware at most of the local restaurants has been made by a neighborhood potter, with the same effect.

If your business deals in a product or service useful to a narrow cross-section of the populace, such as a dental ceramics lab, or an executive search firm for chimney sweeps, then you would want to tailor your ad campaign to reach the people who are in need of your business. One way of finding each other is to place ads in, or even be interviewed by, the publications catering to your particular field. Your location may or may not be an issue and, in some cases, rather than advertising its convenience, it may be advisable to restrict your accessibility to a mailing address.

For businesses that would benefit from mass-market advertising, the objective is to consider the widest range of media visible—or audible—

to the people you serve. Consider them all carefully, from local symphony program notes to postcards at tourist shops to radio spots. Direct mail remains a powerful mass medium involving a number of subtle techniques. Most people who do a direct-mail-order campaign are pleased with a 2 or 3 percent response; it's a very tricky business. Seek out the talented, experienced mail-order person in your community. Use the same approach in seeking experienced opinions about display advertising and classified ads. Forget "theories" here, just as in other realms of business. Someone else's experience, over many years, is the best way to understand what works in all types of advertising. Don't limit your learning by restricting your inquiries to people in your own line of work.

In advertising, follow the same guidelines given in Chapters 6 and 8: *start small and go slow.* If you must advertise, run the smallest ad campaign that you can, so you can get feedback from friends, and so that you can *feel* what it's like to have an ad broadcast about you. Most of all, you will find that experimentation is vital to get a sense of all the variables. If you're using a classified ad, try changing the sizes of type, as well as the wording of the copy. If it is a display ad, experiment with the size, design and logo to get a feel for what gets response and what range of visible images you feel comfortable with. In adjusting these factors, never change more than one thing at a time. Decide on the most realistic interval between changes in order to accurately observe and evaluate their impact. Then schedule the changes to allow for that period of delayed reaction so that you can test the effects of each alteration. It's fine to run an ad, or a group of ads, in different media and locations, but make sure that you can measure the results of each ad, either with special sale coupons, or by asking customers what drew them to you.

Slowly paced change is vital to determine the value of each particular ad in paying for itself. The Owner-Builder Center, a group that runs classes to teach people how to build their own homes, ran a display ad in a variety of newspapers and asked people, upon enrollment, where they learned about it. This approach was fairly successful in pinning down which medium got the best return. The big successes were very clear. They experimented with varying the type face and dimension, and developed a very effective format.

C. C. Hoge, Sr., in his book *Mail Order Moonlighting,** makes a strong point. "The apparent difference between overpoweringly effective ad-

* 10 Speed Press, Berkeley, CA, 1976.

vertising and ineffective advertising is far slighter than most people have any inkling. Again and again, seemingly slight variations have made the difference. . . . In an inch ad, just putting a thick dotted line border will sometimes improve results 20 percent or more . . . bigger type in a headline can make a 35 percent or more difference." Hoge also says never to rest on your laurels, ads can always be improved.

Yellow Pages ads can be very important for some businesses, and inconsequential for others. For this reason, it is difficult to give good general advice on these ads. Sometimes they are such an important source of clientele that it is not worth starting your business until you can be listed in the phone directory.

First look in the *Yellow Pages* at ads for businesses similar to yours. If other, similar businesses run large ads, wonder why they do that and consider the financial implications. Check all separate headings under which your business can be listed, and decide which ones to try. The rate of making and monitoring experimental changes in these ads will be much slower than for display and classified ads, because the directories are issued only once a year. If you are in an area where there are a number of different phone directories, you have more opportunities to experiment. Do so.

Anxiety

"What do I do about the anxiety I feel while I'm starting my business?" It is very common for people to have great anxiety about their business—waiting for it to break even, to cover the rent and to make ends meet. For some people, the anxiety over being self-generating—of not having someone else tell you what to do—is acute, something they failed to anticipate.

The level of and reasons for anxiety that people have varies greatly from person to person. For this reason, it is hard for others to understand our particular anxiety. It is still harder for other people to help us deal with it.

For Michael, confronting the maximum level of anxiety that he believed to be tolerable, a level that felt like the edge of a nervous breakdown, resulted in calm and tranquility.

He said, "My personal encounter with intense anxiety occurred two months after I left a salaried job as a bank vice-president. For those two months I had been working extensive hours at a hectic pace, meeting the demands of a new and growing clientele of people who wanted me as a business consultant. The anxiety reached its peak when I was at sea, on a cruise ship, leading a team of researchers. I felt totally isolated and overwhelmingly burdened. There was nothing for me to do but lie down and cry. I cried for hours. When I stopped crying, I was overcome with a total calmness. I was sitting in a deck chair covered with warm blankets. I didn't move for twenty-four hours, the tranquility was complete. From that point on, my confidence and strength grew steadily. The anxiety was gone, the power to deal with all my problems was readily available.

"That level of anxiety has never returned, but if it does I will seek the isolation that works for me. In that isolation, I will confront the anxiety and surrender to it."

Our friend Charles Albert confronted a similar anxiety when he left a job. He started a counseling business that grew very slowly. For an entire year, he watched his savings dwindle. When he reached his last $200, he panicked. He was the sole supporter of his young son, and his $300 rent was past due. Charles Albert went through the same terror-then-calm experience that Michael had, and found his anxiety replaced by tranquillity. With the new calmness he could think clearly and solve problems day-by-day, as they came up. The disappearance of his energy-draining anxiety left him with new energy to find odd jobs, earning $10 to $20 at a time, to pay the rent, and to systematically build up his counseling business.

What Rasberry does is imagine the worst possible consequence that could occur, surrendering to her most gruesome fantasies. Somehow accepting and giving in to her fears allows them to dissipate.

The lesson from our experience is that intense anxiety is debilitating. Confront it, surrender to it and seek the calmness that follows.

Apprentice

If you take on an apprentice, or apprentice yourself to someone in order to learn their business, it is vital to write down all of your mutual expectations. Learning is what apprenticeship is about, and teaching is offered in lieu of wages, or in partial payment. It is important to understand what each person wants, needs and expects from the apprenticeship. Once you've discussed your expectations, write them down.

If your business is short on cash, and you are long on patience and time, then consider taking on an apprentice to help you. This tradition is important and worthwhile for all of us to support in all fields of business, especially when we are running an honest business.

Artists in Business

A common dinner discussion we have these days is with artists and craftspeople who just can't "make it." This kind of despair over making a living through their art or craft is quite common, and is heard from weavers, potters, singers, painters and jewelry makers.

More than in any other category of business, artists and craftspeople need to make a realistic appraisal of their tradeskill ability. Being an accomplished designer does not guarantee that you are a clever businessperson. Neither does being artistic mean you are *not* capable of running your own business.

It used to be a popular pose for artists to be naïve and easily manipulated concerning the business side of their work. Many artists and craftspeople have become sophisticated in acknowledging their tradeskill, if they have it, and go on to succeed in business. If they don't have tradeskill, they find a partner who does.

Artists *can* make a living from their work if they are: 1. good at what they are doing, 2. willing to work full time at it for a year, and 3. pay attention to the business aspects of their work.

Bess Bair, a great tap dancer and teacher, was able to make a living at her art within one year from the time she decided to be businesslike about it. She had been teaching small classes of three to seven students, several days a week, and periodically performing on the streets and at night clubs, where she passed the hat. Bess supplemented her small tap dance earnings by teaching classes in auto repair for women.

When she decided to make a serious business of her teaching and performing, she prepared a financial statement and made income projections for the coming year. These she took to a bank, where she borrowed $1,000 to install a small tap dance floor in her studio. From her projection, she knew how many students and how many classes she needed to repay the loan and earn the monthly income she wanted. With this goal in mind, she set out to do it with all the techniques that she knew, from past experience, would work. Classified ads, posters and phone calls to current and former students were her prime methods of generating business.

Most importantly, she did a brilliant publicity job. Bess tap danced across the Golden Gate Bridge on Labor Day and set a tap dancing distance record for the *Guinness Book of World Records.* She also took her students to a variety of public places and did many free performances. Within a year, the tap dance classes had a waiting list of students and Bess was being paid in advance for night club performances and private parties.

Betsy is another example. She had been selling quilts that she made and working part time at other things. Her quilts are very delicate and take a long time to make. She had been slowly selling them for six years and now wanted to make a living at it.

Together we went over her records, which were in good shape. She made a list of all her past clients, as well as of galleries and stores that had sold her work. This, then, was her community, where her future sales would come from. She quit her part-time jobs, then meticulously arranged a series of shows and private parties to display her work. She invited everyone in her community, phoning them individually to follow up on written invitations. Even though Betsy was a very shy person, at every show she carefully made a point of talking to each person. The methodical qualities that showed in her quilts were relevant to her business. Sales and commissions for works of art grew slowly, month by month, until Betsy was supporting herself as a quilt artist within a year.

Mimi Manning had been working for two years at a part-time job, and spending the rest of her time doing the batik and paper dyeing work that she loved. The batik and paper business had produced a monthly income for her that ranged from nothing to $500. She was tired of the part-time job because it didn't leave her enough time for her art. The rationale she gave herself for continuing the part-time job was that she could save up the money to buy a sizable inventory of supplies and have the cash to get her through enough months to build up the business.

The facts were that she had been doing the part-time job for two years, and she still didn't have the money saved, nor did she have the energy to build the business. Mimi took the bold step of quitting her job, started working hard at the business, and she made it. It now supports her.

If you can't make a living at your art or craft, then reexamine the issues: are you uniquely good at what you're doing? Have you devoted your full energy over a long enough period to make it work? Have you treated it as a serious business?

Bankruptcy and Liquidation of a Business

Closing a business is as much a part of the business life cycle as beginning one. With the advent of corporations in the last century, it is less common for people to think of closing as a natural part of the cycle. But all businesses die. Most of them last only a few years or decades, some last beyond a lifetime, and one out of a million will last for over a century. Many of the corporations that seem to have lasted that long are actually *names* that survive; the businesses that were the ancestors to the present companies either came to the end of their cycle and sold the name, or evolved through structural modifications. For instance, General Motors is a conglomerate of dozens of dying corporations that it bought. As with all things, there is a time for a business to die.

A business's death throes are sometimes disguised by the phrase: "We need a lot of fresh capital." In other cases, the owner is tired or bored.

There are three main ways to close a business. Sell it, liquidate it or abandon it. Selling includes merging with another business, liquidating includes bankruptcy, and abandoning includes jumping out of a high window.

Selling a business is like selling anything else. Sometimes you will have a business no one else wants. There is a market for the sale and purchase of businesses and there are people who specialize in that market. You can advertise in the *Wall Street Journal*, on telephone poles or anywhere else that's appropriate. You can hire a broker to act as a go-between. Chances are that any of these routes will lead you to a broker, especially an ad in the *Wall Street Journal*, which might yield you twenty letters from brokers.

Pricing a business is difficult. It boils down to a bidding issue, often based on how much you'll finance and what you'll accept as collateral for payment. Most frequently, the leading person in a sizable business will have to sign an agreement to stay on and run it for a few years and frequently that person is prohibited from starting anything competitive for some time.

Liquidating a business is a very surprising thing. Most people think that if they can't pay all their suppliers, they are supposed to go into bankruptcy. That is rarely the case. Even when the company has a negative net worth (it owes more than it owns), liquidation can be very smooth and straightforward. Liquidation means that you sell everything the company owns and pay off as much of the debt as you can. In many areas of the country there are firms that specialize in liquidating businesses, large and small, that are outside the realm of court-ordered liquidation. Some are nonprofit and take only a small percentage—10 percent of the final sale price has been the fee in the cases where we have been involved.

The first step in closing a business with a negative value (called voluntary liquidation) is to assemble all your creditors to present them with up-to-date and accurate financial information, and to answer all their questions. If they trust you and your liquidator to give them each a proportionate share of the business's remaining assets, then you go ahead and do just that.

Throughout all phases of the liquidation procedure, there are three things to keep in mind:

First: at any time, one or more of your creditors can request a court to appoint a liquidator. This action imposes "involuntary liquidation." When you receive a legal summons to that effect, then you need a lawyer. Occasionally it is possible, when a court handles the bankruptcy for you, to continue running the business and trying to get out of debt. This is rarely done but legally possible. You can also ask a court to protect your assets while liquidating your business. This expensive alternative is called "voluntary bankruptcy," and may be warranted where complexities include family, partners and inheritance.

Second: voluntary liquidation of assets should proceed in the same manner as it would if conducted by a court. The order of satisfaction of liens is: direct and withholding taxes first, wages second and secured debt third. The holders of secured notes are usually banks. You distribute to everyone else equally. The owners and the shareholders are at the end of the line. If you violate this order, such as paying yourself or your friends first, expect trouble. Lots of it.

Third: certain debts, for example federal withholding taxes, are not absolved upon the death of a business. These can not only remain after the bankruptcy and liquidation of the business, but also can be charged against any personal assets remaining after a personal bankruptcy. The same principle applies to back wages, including overtime and vacation pay. The whole point is: if the business is marginal and getting near the end of its life, or even in a precarious situation, make sure that there are enough assets left to cover withholding taxes and wages.

Declaring personal bankruptcy is not necessarily part of a business liquidation. There are many cases in which the owner has liquidated the company and gone on to do something else without going through personal bankruptcy, even though the company has not paid off all its debts. This situation is not uncommon if the creditors feel that the owner has been truthful and has done everything possible to help them. Creditors in such cases will forgive the rest. However, in instances where the owner has sizable personal assets, visible or suspected, the creditors can force a personal bankruptcy in hopes of getting the owner to sell those assets to pay off the business debts.

Banks, Banking, Loans

From Michael's years as a banker, his main counsel is that when bankers are secretive, mysterious or obscure about some banking issue, it is because they don't know what they are doing. There are good bankers, incompetent ones and the remaining 90 percent. Good bankers can and will explain to you what they know, and tell you when they don't know.

Banks, and branches within banks, differ greatly in the competence, quality of service and skills they offer. Look around before choosing your bank and branch. If your business is in a specialized field, phone around and find the bank branch that has the greatest familiarity with that field. Since most people don't believe that a great difference exists, you will not get much help. Persist. Arrange for introductions to bankers, and ask people in administrative positions in banks about which of their branches know your field. When you succeed in locating a promising bank, introduce yourself to the manager. When you open your account, use the largest deposit possible, even if you have to borrow the money from a friend and return it to your friend the next day. Even though we are now in the last quarter of the twentieth century, bankers are still influenced by the "opening balance" of an account, a vestige of nineteenth-century banking practices.

A very friendly banker, especially a personal friend, can be helpful in many ways. The most useful would be an awareness of the local business climate, of unusual practices that work for other businesses and of impending loans in your area or field that may have an influence on your business. Even if you aren't close friends, a helpful banker can show you how to avoid nonsensical red-tape procedures followed by the other bank officers.

Getting a Loan from a Bank

Banks are not interested in any form of risk. No risk. If you are asking for a loan for a venture offering less than 100 percent certainty of re-paying the loan, plus interest, then don't bother with a bank.

If you need such a loan and want a bank to finance it, then think of some way to make it 100 percent secure for the bank, such as offering collateral or finding a co-signer who has assets.

Collateral is anything the bank can VERY EASILY sell or move from one account to another, such as a savings account.

A co-signer is someone who will easily repay the loan if, for ANY REASON, you don't.

Banks don't take risks. They occasionally make mistakes, which is why a loss rate on loans of greater than 0.4 percent—that is, four tenths of one percent—is terribly embarrassing to them.

Banks are not the place to go for a loan when starting a business. You might want to go to them when you need to finance new equipment, buy more inventory, pay off some demanding creditors, if you need cash in an off-season, or when other people owe you more money than you can afford to finance for them. Don't bother to apply if you can't meet the ideal of no risk.

When applying for a loan, it's best to have a long history of trans-actions with the bank, which is why choosing the bank carefully in the first place matters and why meeting the manager matters. It even helps to have applied for a business loan before and been turned down. A banking history contributes to the idea that you DO exist, and have existed in the past, and will exist in the future to pay off the loan with interest.

The ideal loan application should be very, very neat, even bound, if you can do that without feeling too formal.

Page one of your loan application is a letter introducing yourself and stating in bankers' language why you want the loan. Bankers' language involves such terms as "secured note," "note on accounts receivable," "equipment loan," etc.

Page two is a detailed account of your business skill and the history of your business.

Page three, for most small businesses, is a list of the names and phone numbers of creditors and suppliers with whom you have a good record. This list includes the phone company, the utility company and your land-lord.

Page four is a list of your clients and/or related business references.

Next is your up-to-date financial statement, along with any necessary explanations, and your prior year's income tax statements, also with an explanation.

Nearly last is your projection of future income, which must demonstrate why you are certain that there will be sufficient net income to repay the loan with interest.

Occasionally, the bank will want a detailed list of your receivables and of equipment that you own.

Last, find some way to have this loan application package individualize your particular business. Remember that it's going to sit on someone's desk for days and possibly go before a committee of people you'll never meet. One artist put a photo of her work and color samples on the last page. A restaurateur included his menu and a secret recipe. A publisher sent a set of recent books that his company had published. Find something similar to these unique touches that will make life more interesting for your banker and the loan review committee—and will help you get a loan.

Barter

Many businesses accept a trade of goods and services in lieu of money. This is called barter. The amount of barter in business has been increasing in the past decade, probably because it is a way to avoid taxation. There are several companies around the United States that act as barter banks and brokers. There are also individuals who barter for ideological reasons, trying to find alternatives to money.

We find that *personalized barter* with customers and with suppliers is beneficial. Barter through clubs or barter banks is a different matter and should be evaluated the same way as credit cards. Decide whether the additional business covers the added costs and is the type of business you want.

The first benefit of personalized barter is that it encourages stronger, more intimate relations with customers and suppliers. The discussions that surround the barter transaction allow many opportunities to talk about personal lives, friends and social topics. The end product of barter is the development of friendships and mutual appreciation that are more difficult to foster in a cash transaction.

The second benefit is that it broadens the lives of the business people involved in the barter. If we see our customers only as a source of money, we have too narrow a view of them. Being open to barter means learning about people and their lives. It also encourages people to think about the reasons they are in business and about their working conditions. A lawyer we know accepted barter of motorcycle parts in return for legal services. Her motorcycle was slowly modified by her client and, before long, she was entering moto-cross races with it and had a loyal cash paying client. Her own work and avocation became much closer.

If you are asked to barter for your goods and services, an effective response is to ask the other person to make a list of six barter options from which you can select one. We do this occasionally in lieu of cash for small-business consulting. As of this writing, we have written options good for a six-person dinner in New York City and another one good for a weekend's use of a private home on the Northern California sea coast.

Many people in America today are experiencing the benefits and joys of bartering. We are placing a higher value on our goods and services than on the dollar they represent. In some cases, our reasons are ideological, but in many situations bartering is just plain horse sense. In the country, bartering is a way of life, a fresh head of lettuce or an egg still warm from the hen just can't be beat. A community is created through bartering and, to country people, community is crucial. Bartering is not limited to small towns, and many small businesses and individuals are happy to exchange with you. The possibilities are unlimited and include your doctor, dentist, lawyer, babysitter, gardener, car mechanic, bread maker, barber—whatever you need or want, consider trading for it.

Better Business Bureau

Small businesses are often asked to join the Better Business Bureau. The BBB is a sad farce. If this organization, which has member groups around the country, had been of any value in the last fifteen years, the whole consumer movement wouldn't have grown so large. If your city or town has a consumer union, or similar activist organization, it's because the BBB is useless. They have absolutely no law enforcement powers and can't force a business to reimburse you even if you have been cheated.

Even if they had power to deal with a business that was cheating the public, how could we expect an organization that is supported by business membership fees to effectively police businesses for very long? The BBB has been around for a long time—too long.

Chamber of Commerce

Some Chambers of Commerce are good, some wonderful and many are neither. Check around to see what your local group has done in the previous few years. If nobody knows, that's a good clue.

Closing a Business (see Bankruptcy)

Collecting on Overdue Bills

We assume that you keep close track of people and businesses that owe you money, that you bill promptly, that the terms of your invoice are clear and that you remind customers if their payment is late. Having done all of that, what can you do when invoiced payments are overdue?

Most small businesses have a real advantage in collecting past-due bills. While a large business has the power to cut off sales until the customers pay their bills, the small business has the opportunity to use imagination.

Collection is usually a case of persuading the slow payer to pay your bill ahead of others. Others trying to get their bills paid customarily use intimidating tactics. Tailor your approach to the particular customer. Most collectors use the phone. When possible and convenient, you should visit the customer. When using the phone, politely involve as many people at the delinquent business as possible in the discussion of late payment.

You can offer your services in helping other people earn the money they owe you. In one case, a small retailer who was owed money by another retail business joined forces to hand out flyers on a downtown street corner. In another case, a film distributor made some social contacts in his town for an out-of-town theater operator who was far behind in a payment. In both instances, the personal service got the bills paid.

If you have a really recalcitrant person to deal with, you can offer to accept a barter for the amount of your bill. The hope is that you will find something you can use and, at the very least, something to accept for barter that you can, in turn, sell.

You can also offer to accept one of your delinquent client's receivables in payment for the bill. In such a case, you look through the accounts receivable of your client to see if there are any of his receivables that are your suppliers. If there are, then you can trade bills. For example, you visit Hindy's coffee shop that bought $350 worth of pastry from your bakery three months ago and never paid. You learn that that coffee shop regularly delivers sandwiches to Jill's print shop, which does your printing. You encourage the coffee shop to extend credit to the print shop for $350, and then give you the bill. You then cancel your bill with the coffee shop (don't extend credit to them again) and use the coffee shop bill as credit on future printing at the print shop.

Just being willing to go to this much trouble will usually keep you in good graces with your late-paying customers. It is nearly always less trouble to be helpful than belligerent, and more effective than going to small claims court.

In an honest, open business it is reasonable to post information about slow-paying customers, so long as you post the same kind of information about your own business practices. One of the advantages is the number of suggestions people make to you about how to handle collection problems. Often the suggestions are good, and more often people will help you in difficult cases with pertinent information.

Consignment (see Memo)

Co-ops (see Corporation)

Copyrights, Trade Names, Service Marks and Trademarks

These words represent a potential quagmire of problems. Copyrights are useful for printed material, music and works of art, if you aren't making too many separate items (because each registration costs money). With a copyright, you control the legal rights to reproduce your work. No one else can do so without your consent.

There are three important things to realize about registration for any of these forms of protection: the application must be filed precisely according to the latest law or you will have wasted your time; you must follow explcit procedures and terminology when giving others permission to use your property (that means you can't carelessly ignore some infringements and seek to enforce the rest); lastly, even with registered rights, your only real power is the power to sue someone else. That costs YOU money. If you sue, you have to prove at the time of the court hearing that your certificate is the first one registered. You often can't demonstrate that without a great deal of expense. All this leads to the advice that, before you apply for any kind of protection, you should ask other people in your line of business what their experience has been. That way you will find out what they have done, and why they did it (or what they have not done, and why they wish they had). Then, with that array of facts written down, ask a lawyer who has had a minimum of ten years' experience in this field what his or her advice is.

The one instance where we've seen a copyright registration play a substantial role involved Robert Crumb, a cartoonist whose unique character, Mr. Natural, was copied with the motto "Keep on Truckin'" and reproduced on tens of thousands of artifacts without his permission. A lawyer undertook the case "on spec" in return for a large percentage of the settlement, and after several years succeeded in winning one. Crumb's work was clearly unique, and the extent of the infringement had reached enormous proportions, with a large amount of money involved.

One of the ironies of protective restrictions is that the paranoia surrounding them often isn't justified. In a number of cases we've known, people have originated a product which was then copied by others. The consequence, in each case, was that the infringement created a large new market of customers who bought the original product.

In the numerous studies Michael did as a banker, he found a similar pattern. His bank was the Bank of California, and a much larger competitor was the United California Bank. Customers and noncustomers were both quite confused about the bank names. However, whenever either bank did extensive advertising or promotion, both banks got more customers and inquiries. Both benefited from the confusion and got more value for both their own and each other's advertising than did other banks not sharing similar names.

Corporation

Should you incorporate your business? There are four alternatives to incorporation: form a cooperative, operate a muddle, be a sole proprietor or become a partnership.

If you are a cooperative, you already know it and may only want legal status. Contact the Cooperative League, U.S.A., and the Community Services Administration, in Washington, D.C., for lots of free published material. There are producer co-ops, distributor co-ops and retail co-ops. All receive significant tax advantages and many are eligible for low-cost loans. Some of the largest businesses in this country are agricultural co-ops.

The order of business organization, from simplest to most complex, is from muddle to sole proprietorship to partnership to corporation. If you start a business without taking any formal action, you have a muddle. When you (or someone you work with) files a Schedule C attached to your federal income tax return, you have a sole proprietorship. When you have a verbal agreement among the people with whom you are working, and these people attach a partnership return to their federal income tax, then you have a partnership. Finally, when you apply to the State Corporation Commissioner, or the equivalent in your state, to form a corporation, and pay the appropriate fees, you are a corporation. What are the advantages and disadvantages of each type of organization?

A *muddle* can be very useful for a group of people starting a business when they don't clearly know what they want to do or how well they work together. The muddle form allows a great deal of room to experiment, and the opportunity to make major changes without consulting a lawyer or bickering over tax implications.

In a typical muddle, three people with similar skills work on a few jobs together to see if their ideas work. Herb, an experienced floor refinisher, Lew, a painter, and Lorie, a Jill-of-all-trades, got a contract to refurbish a house for a mutual friend of theirs. They agreed to call their relationship a muddle, because of all the uncertainties of working together and coming out of the venture with a net profit. In the end, they decided not to take on another job together. Lorie went to work for Herb as an employee in his floor sanding business, where he was a sole proprietor.

In another instance, three men worked together for nearly fifteen months on a variety of carpentry projects, calling their relationship a muddle until they decided to form a partnership because they had learned that they were comfortable working as a group, and that their skills were complementary.

The specific disadvantage of a muddle is that it is not useful where a lot of money or equipment is involved, because the only form of ownership it allows, without creating problems, is for separate members of the muddle to own separate things.

A muddle is a good, initial step in a business in many instances, but it should not be allowed to survive very long. When a clear decision to create another business form is possible, act on it. If not, every six months you should examine the reasons why a clear decision is still not possible.

A *sole proprietorship* exists when one person (or a married couple) runs a business and files a tax statement for the business as part of his or her own personal tax return.

A *partnership* is in effect when more than one person is in business, and the people have an agreement about their mutual roles. In terms of taxes, the partners each file a financial statement for the total business, stating their share of the business and showing their share of the income or loss on their own taxes.

In a partnership, there can be two kinds of partners: general and limited. The general partners are those people who work in the business and make decisions. The limited partners are those who contribute money or other assets, but don't play a role in operating or deciding about the business. The limited partners are called such because they have "limited" legal liability if a lawsuit is brought against the business. Usually, they have no personal liability for the actions of the business, and stand to lose only the money or assets that they invested in the business. For more details, see Partnership on pages 154–56.

A *corporation* is a legal structure that has a lot of regulatory and tax complexity associated with it, and plenty of paperwork. You can form a corporation in most states for less than $1,000 in legal and filing fees. In many states you can find books on the subject, and do it yourself by paying the several hundred dollars in filing fees. But do you want to?

Most business people make a choice between sole proprietorship, partnership and corporation. There are plenty of each of these around, which is evidence that each form has some advantages.

A corporation has some very specific advantages:

1. Its liability protection for owners, especially in those fields where similar insurance liability protection is too expensive (see below for details).
2. Some pension plan benefits for doctors and other professionals that are derived from federal tax laws are available only to corporations.
3. Unlike a partnership, the method for dissolving a corporation doesn't have to be thought about in advance. The corporation either liquidates everything when it goes out of business, and distributes the surplus to shareholders in proportion to their stock holdings, or when a shareholder wants to leave the company, he or she need only sell the shares held to someone else—much easier than leaving a partnership.

See Partnership and Nonprofit for other considerations.

Common Myths Regarding Incorporation

Many people believe that the prime advantage of the corporate form is that the owner or owners are legally better protected from the liabilities of the business than are general partners or sole proprietors. It is believed that in a lawsuit, the owners of the corporation have a better chance of avoiding personal liability. Actually:

1. Limited partners in a partnership have nearly the same protection as owners of a corporation.
2. Insurance is available to protect general partners and sole proprietors in liability suits. The rates differ with the circumstances, but it is a frequently used alternative to forming a corporation.
3. The corporation has to be careful in its record keeping and its transactions, especially if it is a small business. It is possible for the prosecution in a liability suit to disregard the corporate entity and sue individual owners in cases where the corporation is not well run. This can occur where there are inadequate board minutes; self-dealing transactions; and questionable pension plans.
4. Most banks and lenders to small corporations require that the principals in the business sign personal guarantees on all corporate loans. This measure completely negates the corporate protection to owners in terms of loan liabilities.

There are more disadvantages to incorporating. There is lots more paperwork for a corporation to file with state and federal governments; there are unique ways directors of a corporation can be sued and held accountable other than in straight liability suits; and there is a high tax rate on the business if its net profits are over $25,000.

Corporate taxes start out high and rise to the 50 percent rate. To avoid this high rate, there is a corporate form called Sub-Chapter S, available to small corporations with few shareholders. Sub-Chapter S allows a corporation to be treated, in tax terms, like a partnership or sole proprietorship. Consult a good accountant for details.

See Partnership and Nonprofit for other considerations.

Credit Cards

Many people who own small businesses don't personally use general purpose credit cards. General purpose cards include Visa, Mastercard and American Express.

As a consequence, it is not unusual to find small retail stores that don't accept any credit cards. The personal feelings of the owners are sometimes backed up by rudimentary research, in which a count is made of the number of customers who ask "Do you take credit cards?" The number of such questions is then compared to an estimate of the lost business. The finding, in some cases, is that the loss is less than the percentage charge that the credit card companies levy the business. The problem with this logic is that it doesn't measure the number of customers who don't ask about using their cards, and excludes any measurement of the customers who buy more when credit cards are an acceptable form of payment.

Nearly all small retail business experience has been in support of credit cards. More customers buy when cards are accepted, and they spend more money. Credit cards offer small businesses a credit service that would be too expensive for them to operate individually. Sales nearly always go up more than enough to pay their cost.

Credit cards are a service to the customers, especially those who feel uncomfortable carrying cash for fear of theft or loss through carelessness.

Employees

If you have a business that can avoid having employees, don't hire any. This is the most frequent advice given to sole proprietors, and it is the most often ignored. Employees nearly always have far greater emotional cost in these circumstances than they warrant. The alternatives are part-time helpers, independent contractors or spouses. Employees entail supervision and paperwork. Make sure you have a grasp of how much each of these cost in terms of your time and satisfaction before you take on employees.

Withholding Taxes on Employees

Many small businesses attempt to skirt paying withholding taxes for employees by calling them independent contractors. The definition of "independent contractor" is clearly spelled out in our tax laws. It is a mistake to misinterpret the legal definition of independent contractor for too long. If you have real employees, then admit it to yourself and the IRS. If you have employees, be sure to do the tax withholding. There are two strong reasons.

First, if the business goes under or goes through bankruptcy, the withholding tax liability will still exist and haunt you indefinitely. Second, the IRS can close your business for this reason, without any hesitation or delay on their part. They can close it Wednesday night, at 11:25, if you have failed to do employee income tax withholding and the IRS has reason to suspect that your business doesn't have sufficient assets to pay them.

If it is ambiguous whether the people who work for you are employees or independent contractors, then apply three simple tests:

1. Do you provide them with all or most of the tools they work with?
2. Are they under your direct supervision?
3. Are your payments to them more than three-quarters of their annual income?

"Yes" to any two means they are considered your employees by the IRS. You have a good chance of getting caught and having to pay their back taxes.

Your chances of getting caught are not directly related to anything the IRS does to find you, but is usually the result of a well-meaning, friendly ex-employee who applies for unemployment payments or medical payments for job-related problems. That type of action alerts the IRS.

If you want to avoid the withholding tax, form a partnership that includes your employees. Then the employees pay their own taxes.

Bruce, a painting contractor, formed a partnership with his five painters. He controlled the partnership at the outset, but the longer his painters stayed with him, the more power they acquired. He also had simple provisions to buy their share of the partnership for fixed amounts if they quit or were kicked out. In this way, he avoided paying withholding taxes. His five partners filed their individual copy of the partnership return (see Partnership).

See Chapter 10 for a discussion of some of the other issues regarding the withholding of employees' income taxes, and Chapter 13 for issues of management relations with employees.

Ending a Business (see Bankruptcy)

Exclusive Rights

It might appear that giving exclusive rights to sell something and giving an exclusive territory to a distributor are beneficial to almost any business.

However, exclusiveness *is not beneficial* for a business that practices openness and believes in service as its primary objective.

There are two traditional reasons for creating such exclusive territories. One is that the dealer with exclusive rights will work harder because the exclusiveness is an incentive to promote the product. If two nearby dealers have the product, it is traditionally assumed that neither would do as much promoting because the other would get part of the benefits. The second is that a higher price is possible where there is less competition. The first traditional reason is generally false and the second is generally true.

Most exclusive dealers seem to get lazy and don't do much. If the product sells itself, wonderful; if it doesn't, then "Why pour good money after bad?" they say. Good contracts and ingenious incentives seldom seem to have an effect. If the product is good, it DOES sell. They are right. From your point of view, if it sells, then it will sell better with more distributors, not fewer.

On the second point, exclusive rights do seem to lead to higher prices. Is that what you want? The alternative is to have more stores and representatives carrying the product so more people can learn about it and find it in more convenient locations. Your price would be lower without exclusive rights, but your potential for more sales, and thus more profit, would be greater with a variety of distributors.

"Exclusive" is a business word for greed and paranoia. In reality it doesn't work for honest businesses. Most products benefit as more people participate in the sales processes.

It is interesting to compare RCA's development of the 45-rpm record system in the mid-1950s and Philips Corporation's development of the cassette cartridge in the 1960s.

RCA tried the exclusive approach, with their machine the only one on the market that could play their tiny 45-rpm discs. Outcome: limited turntable sales, heavy promotional and development costs.

Philips's cassette technology, by contrast, was licensed to nearly anybody who wanted it. The product completely overran its two predecessors, reel-to-reel tapes and 8-track cartridges. It is a great success story for openness in business licensing.

Lawyers

In this book we have occasionally recommended the use of a lawyer. Lawyers can be helpful as consultants for a small, open business, and where an issue is extremely important, several lawyers should be sought for consultation.

However, every effort should be made to avoid using lawyers when you are angry or disappointed. The use of lawyers and courts to try and accomplish some business end, where the lawyers are your hired mercenaries, is nearly always a losing situation. Most people aren't experienced enough to use lawyers as mercenaries: they hire them as demigods who are expected to win some justice or revenge for them. But even hired as mercenaries, the cost of waging legal battles is nearly always far greater than the winnings or settlements of cases. This should be obvious from the behavior of casualty insurance companies, who try never to resort to lawyers and courts in settlements.

The alternatives to lawyers and legal battles are negotiation and arbitration. In many situations that we've seen, where friction was great and animosity was high, both parties were willing to find a negotiator or an arbitrator to work with in avoiding a costly legal battle.

A negotiator is anyone, or any group, that helps both sides together to find a mutually agreeable solution. An arbitrator is a person who is agreed upon by both sides to actively direct a settlement. Arbitrators can be retired business people, ministers, therapists and members of the American Arbitration Society; even lawyers can be used as arbitrators. We like to suggest arbitrators who are wise and respected members of the business community, and chose ours because we held their opinion of us in such high esteem that we would go to great lengths to avoid using their services.

Loans (see Banks)

Marketing Plan

The phrase "marketing plan" has a magic connotation in many business textbooks and courses in business. If you have a "marketing plan," you supposedly have an important key to successful business. The words seem to frighten many people who are starting out in business, because it is hard to understand what a marketing plan is, and once you have one, you aren't sure you really have what the books tell you you should have.

The reason for this problem is that the phrase "marketing plan" is a vague notion that can't be adequately defined so that one serious businessperson can follow directions and make a marketing plan and another serious businessperson can recognize it when it is finished.

Instead of "marketing plan," substitute the phrase, "two-year budget projection with explanations." Nearly everyone in business can tell you how to do this, and recognize one when it is done. Most of all, those people can realistically appreciate how unreliable such a projection can be in the real world.

The purpose of such a two-year projection is to force you to be explicit about your business assumptions. In order to estimate revenues, you must consider who will buy how much, at what price and when. In order to project expenses, you have to visualize your staff, overhead, supply and capital needs. Even the most rudimentary projections will help to make visible the "vital ratios" and the "cash flow."

The vital ratios are the numerical relationships that change at different levels of sales. If you project sales in the fourth month of $10,000 and overhead of $2,000, and you project sales in the twelfth month of $20,000 with overhead of $4,200, then you have a ratio of overhead to sales that is increasing. A bad sign.

Cash flow is the actual cash that the business will have during the projected period. This is important because most businesses have serious problems with it. As business and sales increase, the need for more inventory and supplies increases, at a similar rate. If you sell 400 tofu kits in one month, with an inventory of 200 of them and $6,000 worth of raw material, then if you sell 600 kits the next month you may need an inventory of 300 kits and $11,000 worth of raw material. The problem is that you often have to pay for the inventory and raw materials *before* you get paid for the final products you sell. The problem of cash flow gets worse as sales increase.

Helping you foresee these kinds of problems is the reason to make a two-year budget projection before starting a business.

Memo

Shipping "on memo" is an interesting way to avoid some of the problems of consignment. The idea came to us from *The Crafts Business Encyclopedia*, by M. Scott, (New York: Harcourt Brace Jovanovich, 1977).

When shipping "on memo," you send out an invoice with your product that has a thirty- or sixty-day return privilege. If the product is not returned by then, the invoice is in effect. This is a way to avoid a problem that many crafts artists have in dealing with the issue of consignment versus final sales. By shipping "on memo," their product doesn't sit around in one store too long, and the retailer gets the advantage of having higher-priced goods to display that wouldn't ordinarily be stocked if they had to buy them, and pay for them immediately, on final sales.

Nonprofit

Some business institutions do not have to pay federal or state income taxes. These include churches, schools, some research organizations and charities. These businesses are called "nonprofit" by most people when they casually talk about "nonprofit." However, if you are interested in becoming a nonprofit organization, you need a good understanding of what this matter is really about.

Nearly all so-called nonprofits are corporations that are tax exempt under the 1969 Tax Reform Act, section 501,c.3 and 501,c.4. These are numbers you will run into again and again if you pursue this area of interest. They are so commonly used that nonprofits are occasionally referred to as c3's ("see threes"), because of the section of the law that defines their tax exemption and their required behavior.

There are some nonprofits such as churches, trusts and religious associations that are not corporations. The other nonprofits are all corporations.

Nonprofit corporations always have a unique corporate form, first, before they get their tax exempt status. They are organized, *not to make a profit but to do something specifically for the public good.* In some states they are called "not for profits," in others just "nonprofit" corporations. There are three things that distinguish them from other corporations.

1. Nobody owns shares of stock; no one actually owns the corporation. Nonprofit corporations are controlled by a board of directors.
   No matter how much net surplus income nonprofits generate as a business, that surplus doesn't go to any owners, since there aren't any. The surplus can go back into the business to buy new equipment, to raise salaries or hire more people, or it can be given away to another nonprofit group, or any combination of these things.
2. When a nonprofit goes out of business, the net assets left over after paying all liabilities are turned over to the state where it was incorporated, or given to some other, similar nonprofit corporation.

3. The day-to-day operations of these corporations are subject to special review and penalization by the IRS. There are two things that a tax exempt, nonprofit cannot do that an ordinary corporation can, which will result in penalties directly from the IRS:

a. Executive salaries, loans and transactions between board members, executives and the corporation, political activity, and sources of income are strictly regulated by the IRS to insure that a corporation set up as a nonprofit isn't using that status to further political goals or to line their own pockets.

b. The sources of income to the nonprofit corporation must generally be tied to the stated goals of the corporation, as written in the original articles of incorporation.

An ordinary corporation has a lot of paperwork, but a tax exempt corporation (nonprofit) has more paperwork in its dealings with governmental agencies.

Why would you want to be tax exempt, and what other alternatives are there?

There are two sound reasons that most frequently influence people in choosing a nonprofit as their business form.

First, they get significantly lower postal rates, and in some businesses that can be very helpful.

Second, individuals can make donations to tax exempt nonprofits and usually deduct the gift from their income taxes. Similarly, other "exempt organizations," as they are technically called, can make donations to them.

Like an ordinary corporation, a tax exempt one offers liability protection to its managers and directors.

There is one minor additional value in choosing the nonprofit tax exempt form. They tend to have more public credibility in some fields, such as education, medicine, research and public charity.

However, this same credibility is available in another way. You can be a nonprofit organization in most states, and *not be* tax exempt, if the goals of your business are philanthropic or of an educational or research nature. You just don't apply for an exemption, and you pay taxes like any other corporation, if you earn income that is sufficient to be taxed.

This tax paying form, where you are still a nonprofit corporation, run by a board of directors with no ownership, does not give you any of the advantages listed as three sound reasons for becoming a nonprofit *tax exempt* organization, but it does give you public credibility without all the paperwork and IRS interference.

Partnership (see Corporation)

In the early 1960s, Michael was counseling people who were doing something that later became very common. It is now called "living together." He was concerned about the financial problems involved, particularly the problems for women who had much better protection under the traditional marriage contract. He asked his Uncle John, a powerful and wise lawyer in New York, about it. John said, "Recommend a partnership. A partnership is a divorce agreement signed when the parties involved are still in love."

That is why partnership agreements are extremely helpful and also why they are hard to write. They deal almost entirely with the issues of dissolution of the partnership.

In considering the partnership form for your business, start with the reality that few business relationships between people last more than a year. Still fewer last more than five years, and only rare cases involve working arrangements that last more than ten years.

If you start with this observation, then it makes sense to discuss dissolution of the partnership in advance of it happening. Wills don't make people die prematurely, discussions about partnerships don't destroy a partnership that has any chance of surviving. If discussion of the dissolution actually leads to a dissolution, then you should ask yourselves how workable the partnership would have been.

Most people avoid written partnership agreements because they fear that discussion of the issue of dissolution will end the partnership right away. You can have a partnership based solely on verbal agreements. From the business world's point of view, you have a partnership when you file a partnership return attached to your individual income tax return.

In our experience, verbal partnership agreements are as useful as a book of paper matches under water. It is so easy to remedy this that no excuse has ever made sense. Write down your partnership agreement.

The format is simple for a general partnership (see below). Once you have written it down, a brief, inexpensive visit with a lawyer can make it a very workable document. A limited partnership (see page 145) should also be done by writing it down before taking it to a lawyer, but in that case, there are sufficient complexities so that a lawyer can reasonably charge more.

The format we use in helping people draw up general partnership agreements is:

1. Why is the partnership being formed? Write at least a five-line paragraph describing the reasons for working together and the benefits that are expected. Be as glowing, cheerful, supportive and optimistic as you wish.

2. Tell how decisions are expected to be made, and what alternatives exist if agreement cannot be reached. Consider the possibility of outside arbitrators, mutual friends as well as professionals (check with the American Arbitration Association about their costs).

3. List the assets that each partner brings to the partnership, including skills, money and equipment. You can list these on a separate sheet, "Attachment 1," so that additions can be made to the list as time goes on.

4. Write down expectations about wages paid to partners who work and distribution of net earnings from the partnership.

5. Describe the percentage of the partnership that each person gets. John L. gets 50 percent, Barbara and John C. get 25 percent each. This applies specifically to the way partners show their share of the partnership business on their income tax returns.

   Our experience with shares has been that people should agree on distinct relationships that are reflected in simple numbers: 50–50, two thirds–one third, 75–25, or 90–10 percent. Real relationships between people are not precise enough to warrant the kind of 43.5 percent calculation that some people write into partnerships. In many cases, these finicky figures provoke more arguments than they settle.

6. Last, but MOST IMPORTANT, describe how the assets *and* liabilities of the business will be distributed when:
   a. one or more partners die;
   b. one or more partners want to leave the partnership;
   c. some partners want one or more other partners to leave;
   d. the business fails;
   e. the whole partnership dissolves.

   Consider all the equipment and assets that the partnership will buy over the coming years, and figure out who gets it. Deal with the equipment that people brought into the partnership too.

We worked with some carpenters on a partnership in which the partner who had the most equipment didn't just want his equipment back when the partnership ended, he wanted it back in good condition. The solution was to have him rent his equipment to the partnership, and then pay for the maintenance out of the rental fees.

Take what you've written to a lawyer. The lawyer's role is to ask some questions about points you didn't consider, and write it up for you. The lawyer may also suggest that you record your agreement somewhere, like the local county recorder's office.

Complexity is well suited to the partnership form. If you want to do something that is epecially complex, then write it into the partnership.

Many law firms are able to function with large numbers of partners, sometimes exceeding two hundred, and many levels of partnership responsibility (full, senior, junior, etc.). They can be complex even to the point of spelling out the sizes of desks and credenzas that a partner can have in the office. Of course, they have lawyers around to keep rewriting the partnership agreement at a lower cost than you would have to pay.

Patents (see also Copyrights)

Is getting a patent worthwhile?

The first question is whether you have something that is patentable. The second is whether going through the procedure of applying for a patent will be worthwhile.

Whether you have something patentable can be a very difficult question to answer in many cases. If your "thing" is an object that can be described and manufactured, and it has qualities that are specific enough compared to other, similar objects in the way it is used, then it is probably patentable.

For example, a knife that can be used to cut cheese just as easily as it cuts a slice of white bread could probably be patented if the design were significantly new and unique.

Computer programs, no matter how brilliant or useful, are not patentable, nor are most biological improvements or nitty-gritty sex-aid devices.

The best and least expensive way to answer the question of whether something is patentable is to ask several people in that field who have gotten patents. They are nearly certain to know the answer, unless it falls into some very peculiar area of the law.

In deciding whether to get a patent, there are four problems to consider in advance:

1. If you get a patent in a field of high technology or rapidly changing tastes, you may get it too late to use. You may find that something similar, which does what your product does, was also patented, or that someone else was making and selling your product during the first few years of intense demand. Patents commonly take several years to get, and they do not automatically force other people to stop making the product. Timing can be vital, and slight modifications can make a patent irrelevant.
2. Patent applications are expensive, with a usual $2,000 minimum in legal fees.
3. You have to pay to protect your patent by suing others if they use it. The cost of suing is yours, and you only have a *chance* of collecting your expenses, not a certainty.
4. There are countless patents filed, and only a tiny fraction of them are real products on the market. People often think that a patent is all that is needed to get something made and marketed. It isn't—a patent has little or nothing to do with getting a product on the market.

Generally we have found patents for small businesses to be useless or irrelevant.

What are the alternatives, and when do you want a patent?

One alternative is to pay for a patent search and have a patent attorney make a complete file. Then if you come across someone with a similar invention, you can prove you were the first inventor. The cost is quite low for a patent search, and you have good standing in court if you actually began marketing the product.

Another way, if technology or changing tastes are involved, is to be innovative and stay ahead of the field.

A third way is to hide the secret of your product in some imaginative way. In electronics, it is customary to put the whole device into solid plastic so it becomes hard to find out what the components are. Melting or destroying the plastic destroys the components.

In programming it is customary to build in mazes, trivia and deliberately misleading material, so that someone copying it will have to spend a great deal of time deciphering what is really in the program.

We like the attitude of Ben Franklin, whose inventions included the flexible catheter, the lightning rod, an improved boat hull and the Franklin stove. He refused to patent any of his inventions, believing them to belong to all people. He clearly stated his philosophy, "As we enjoy great advantages from the inventions of others, we should be glad of an opportunity to serve others by any invention of ours."

The specific instance where we find it useful to get a patent is when you have a product for which there is already a proven market, your product is clearly superior to others, has broad applications AND you plan to sell the patent rather than develop it yourself.

Pensions

Pensions can be considered in the light of the ideas expressed in Chapter 16, The Four Illusions of Money.

For a small company with a few employees, a pension plan can best be designed with the help of specialists in the field. That does not mean insurance agents, it means independent firms that can be found in major cities that will provide you with a complete computer list of your alternatives. They charge a fee, but they don't have a hidden agenda to sell.

There is one important thing to keep in mind when thinking of pensions for yourself and when advising employees. Think of nonmonetary alternatives. Use your imagination to find ways that your skills and interests will have a long-term bearing on your life, and particularly the time in your later life when your motor skills are not so good.

Consider being a consultant in the line of business you're in. Start now so you'll have experience in consulting.

If you want to teach, start teaching now. Learn to organize classes by doing the right advertising and promotion (the official teaching world generally closes its doors to teachers at age sixty-five). Give it thought, and think about what experience and skills are necessary. That is what good pension thinking is about.

Under the current Keogh Law that allows self-employed people to set aside savings for a pension, with favorable tax treatment, there are provisions for nonmonetary savings plans. The law requires that your savings be administered by someone else, not you, and that you don't get the proceeds until a specified age (fifty-nine and a half years old).

The object of a good pension plan is to allow you to make use of your present skills, loves and experience when you are older.

Retirement is not discussed here. We don't know clearly what it is. Some people seem to have "retired" at age twenty-four, and others like Bucky Fuller never retire.

Pricing

In some businesses, pricing is really a problem. This is especially true where there is no close substitute for the product or service to use as a guideline.

Finding the right price is a straightforward matter of finding the relationship between what you charge and your Income/Expense Sheet. This takes time and requires your constant attention.

There are two things that we recommend:

1. When pricing something completely new, or new to the market where there is no close competition, look carefully at your costs for the product and then *price it as if you were selling it to your friends.* Pretend a friend asked to buy one, figure out within yourself what price you would charge that person. That should be the price for everyone if you have an open, friendly attitude toward the world. Naturally, you must build in profit or you won't be in business long.
2. Most small-business people we work with charge too little. That is because the estimates of their costs usually understate the amount of time they spend in the business and ignore other elements of overhead such as time on the phone, dealing with mistakes and time spent having fun at work.

When Rasberry began selling crocheted hats she picked a price she thought fair to herself and her customers. Some months later she decided to figure out just how much she earned per hour.

She hung a big poster board on the wall of her workroom and determinedly wrote down every cost related to producing her hats: phone, gas, booth rental, business cards, spinning oil, dyes . . . the list was long.

She also kept track of all the time she spent designing, crocheting, spinning, driving to fairs and dyeing her wool.

Much to Rasberry's chagrin she was earning fifty cents an hour after paying for materials!

Once she could place a realistic dollar value on her work Rasberry was in a position to test the market to see if she could pay herself a living wage and still sell her hats. In her case she wasn't willing to skimp on materials or speed up production so she concentrated on custom orders on which she could be lavish with materials and get paid well for her time.

Fixed price retailing is the unique and recent idea of having a published price for retail products and services available to all customers. Fixed price is distinguished from negotiated price. This practice seems very natural to us, we see prices on most products in department stores, grocery stores and clothing stores. But even into the late twentieth century, we still have negotiated prices for appliances, automobiles and many products and services that cost more than $100. The idea of "one price" seems to have been introduced in the 1850s in the United States, and Alexander Stewart, who created the largest modern department store of his time in Manhattan, is often credited with its innovation. A. T. Stewart & Company advertised, "One price for all." Stewart, himself, claimed a markup of "ten percent and no lies." He was known to fire clerks who reduced prices or overpriced merchandise. By the end of the nineteenth century, fixed prices had become the dominant model for retail business.

Problems

Every business is faced with a wide range of problems—growing too fast or too slow; having personnel who are too demanding or too passive.

There is one piece of general advice that is often useful at times of intense problems and decision making: concentrate your efforts with ⅔ of them going into cost reduction and ⅓ into increasing sales.

This guideline works because cost reduction gives quick results for your efforts, while sales programs take more time. It is also useful because the ways to reduce costs are often more obvious and less risky than sales promotion efforts. But cost reduction usually involves high emotional effort—your working longer hours and others shorter; changing job functions; and having fewer perks for everyone. The advice to put greater effort into cost reduction does not exclude sales promotion as that would be a bad mistake. The advice is, in fact, very conservative, and reflects the ability to minimize risks, an attribute found in people with high trade-skill.

Product Liability Insurance

We assume that people in honest businesses will be exceptionally careful not to manufacture products that might endanger anyone. However, if your business makes or sells a product or service that, by any stretch of the imagination, could result in harm to a buyer, you should think about product liability insurance. Even a beautiful Mylar kite could conceivably fly into a power line and severely shock someone.

Even though you are very careful, sometimes accidents occur. Suppose you are a potter and sold a ceramic pot that explodes in someone's face. You thought it was oven-proof, but their face is horribly scarred. As an honest person, you would be responsible for a good explanation as well as for their expenses. If you feel you can't afford product liability insurance, be sure you *can* afford to care for a customer, if necessary.

No matter how wonderful your product or service, insurance or personal responsibility is essential in business. Of course, the more open you are, the more modest your lifestyle, and the more obvious your interest in serving people, the less likely any issues of product liability are to occur.

Publicity (see also Advertising)

Getting publicity doesn't mean you will get increased sales or that the image you hope to project will come across. The disadvantages of publicity are that:

1. It may get you more inquiries and attention than you can handle. This problem arises when the people who visit and ask questions require more of your attention than you are willing to give. They sometimes have misconceptions and are often not potential customers.
2. Actually getting publicity can be time-consuming and debilitating. Television and radio interviews can be exhausting.
3. You can also get bad publicity, whether you want it or not, simply by seeking publicity in the first place. In giving newspaper and magazine interviews, you should know in advance that you often will be misquoted out of context. You have no control over what

the writer selects to print and often the writer must defer to his or her editor.

Word of mouth is the best way to generate business. New customers from that source are receptive to what you are doing and are, themselves, more willing to continue the word-of-mouth process to wider circles of their friends if they are happy with your business. A publicity-recruited customer is much less likely to do that.

Notwithstanding those drawbacks, you may still want publicity. It is much, much cheaper than advertising, and significantly more effective. This is especially true if your business is open and has service to people as its prime goal. Most media are starved for stories of public interest where someone is trying to help other people. The challenge is to say or enact your message in a way that is newsworthy. That is what publicity is about. When you have figured out what your message or action should be, then you invite the appropriate media to hear, read or watch what you do.

Dealing with the media requires the same degree of experience and wisdom that is required for effectively dealing with courts, IRS investigators, building inspectors, legislatures, rodeo horses and wild mushrooms. Which is to say: get a publicist! We don't know of any books good enough to help you with this. It takes real creativity and good judgment. Also, publicists occasionally have an ongoing and good relationship with the media that is advantageous.

Many publicists want a retainer, so be prepared. Some are willing to work for less if you do the work and they play an advisory role. But you should only accept this kind of relationship if you are sure you have the time and compulsiveness necessary to type press releases, deliver them, phone interviewers for many hours at a time and carry out countless little details.

There are media everywhere for you to work with. Magazines throughout the country are anxious for material, but they want good stories that have something new and interesting about them and that will appeal to their specific readers. If you write an article or have one written about you by a freelance writer, make sure you understand what the magazine you are dealing with considers to be good writing.

In most big cities, the same factors hold true for other media; they want material but only if it meets their standards. If you do a really fine job on a press release, you may be surprised, as we often have been, to find it copied verbatim somewhere you least expected it. We often find it reprinted or read over the air with only tiny modifications. A good press release or press kit should tell a pretty complete story, so that it can be used lock, stock and barrel.

Quality Control

Controlling the quality of your product and service is one of the most important activities of your business if you intend to serve people. Quality control is not obvious, and is not always integrated into a business.

Bob Kahn, a friend of ours, is a great small-business advisor. He publishes the *Kahn Newsletter*, primarily for department stores, from his home in Concord, California. Once Bob took us for a walk near an auditorium where we were both scheduled to speak. He pointed out to us how dirty the fronts of some retail stores were. "To the owners, it's the place they go to work and they forget how it looks to a customer seeing it for the first time."

Quality control means looking at your business through the eyes of a first-time customer.

Manufacturing businesses usually give a lot of thought to quality control; other businesses give less. The problem with service businesses, such as publicists, roommate referrals, dentists and many retail businesses, is that their owners feel uncomfortable finding out how customers respond to their business transactions.

Restaurants usually try to build the evaluation into the business; "Did you enjoy your meal?" asks the maitre d'. The alternative for businesses that don't have this established pattern of quality control is to have the top person, the one who runs the business, periodically contact a random sample of customers and chat with them about their satisfaction with the transaction. This is something that very few businesses that we know of actually do. Even businesses that intend to always seem to put it off.

If you decide to do it, choose several dates during the year in advance and allocate several hours to do the job of interviewing. Then take a good, random sample of your customers so that each person has an equal chance of being chosen. If you have an invoice box, with invoices that are numbered, or a guest register list (number the names), then pick a group of numbers from a random number table (every library, these days, has a random number table, and most statistics books have them in the back) and choose your sample. Phone each person who turns up at the selected number. Ask open-ended questions and ask detailed questions. Use questions such as, "Would the service have been better if we changed something around?" "Were you satisfied with what you bought?" "Would you recommend us to your friends?" "How could we have served you better?"

In two businesses where we know this was done, the customer response was wonderful and the benefits long lasting. The owner, in one case, received a suggestion about the lighting in her restaurant which she immediately incorporated, and in the other case the phoning generated enough energy for the owner to make a major product change in her gallery.

Sex in Small Business

Sex for people in small business requires extra attention. Most people in the initial stages of a business use a lot of their energy and waking hours working hard. In many cases their sexual experiences are reduced during this time. One of the ways to handle this is to acknowledge it regularly. Sex is a field where taboos are so great that couples rarely even discuss it with each other. The common joke about, "I'm sorry dear, I have a headache tonight," is probably an accurate description of most people's sex-related communications. During the time when a business is getting started, it helps to say, "I'm exhausted. If I'm going to get aroused tonight, I'm going to need some attention, a little patience and a massage."

A problem of many small businesses is that the owner/operator spends an enormous amount of time around people involved with the business and may want to have sex with them. The first rule is, don't. Eliminate people you work with, including customers, from your scope of potential sex partners. In fact, a general rule of sex for singles is: don't have sex with people you are geographically close to. That includes neighbors who can see your comings and goings and especially people with whom you work regularly. The unfortunate fact is that one out of five sexual relationships ends with antagonism and sometimes hostility between the partners. Thus, if your business relationship is important, it's not worth the 20 percent chance of jeopardizing that. Otherwise, you may have to quit your job or fire someone or do something drastic that will probably end up to be out of proportion to the sexual rewards in the first place.

For all that, it's important to recognize that, if you're not married, you need to make room in your life to meet potential sex partners, away from the business, and to make a conscious effort to accomplish that.

When you start your own business you should make sure to budget time for your kids, for going to the gym and for your sexual partners as well. Starting a new business often puts strains on intimate relationships. Talk frankly with your spouse or lovers, explain that right now your business is a very high priority and you won't be able to be as spontaneous as usual. Structure time for intimacy. Ask your sexual partners to help create special experiences for you both. Be open. Be imaginative. Many small-business people have developed interesting solutions to this problem. Business is fun and having a vigorous sex life should fit into the business.

Some small-business people take a sex break instead of a coffee break, some have private places available nearby, others encourage long lunch periods and still others rotate traveling sales trips.

Small Business Administration (S.B.A.) and S.B.I.C.

"Can't I go to the S.B.A. for a loan for my business?" That's a very common question with a sad answer.

We have rarely seen a situation where a small, honest business benefited by dealing with the S.B.A. or with an S.B.I.C. (Small Business Investment Corp.). Three outcomes await you, none of them constructive.

In the worst case, you apply for an S.B.A. loan, often through a bank, and then wait for an answer. The application is a monster requiring an enormous amount of time to prepare, and if you are honest about your projections you will have less chance of getting the loan. Then you wait for a response, which can take many months. During that time you have your own anticipation and anxiety to deal with.

Many people we have known didn't do much constructive work during this time period to solve their real problems, they just waited for the BIG GO AHEAD. In nearly all cases we've seen, the answer was "No!" Months were wasted, and time was spent gathering financial data that is now out-dated.

Sometimes S.B.A.s do make a loan or guarantee a bank loan. Usually in these cases they provide no advice or counseling, and forget about the loan until it is in default.

A loan without supervision, advice and concern is often worse than no loan at all. Frequently the loan is for the wrong thing, or when it finally comes, the original need has been resolved and the loan is used for something inappropriate.

In a few cases, a third situation occurs. The small business that needs a loan runs into a broker (usually a former S.B.A. employee) who is in

166 · HONEST BUSINESS

business to guide them through the government labyrinth. The consequence is that the applicant is more likely to get the loan and to get it sooner than through the conventional channels. The trouble is that in order for this to happen, the application is phonied up to make it look more attractive. When the loan comes through, it is totally inappropriate and the way it must be used won't generate the income to pay it back. The result is a desperate scramble for months and sometimes years, to repay the S.B.A. with some other loan that is even more unwieldy.

There must have been some good loans that the S.B.A. and S.B.I.C.s have made somewhere, but we rarely see or hear of them.

There are some interesting programs that the S.B.A. has created. One is called the Small Business Institute, and a related one is called the Small Business Development Center. Both are programs that encourage and fund business school students to work in small businesses while they are students.

Small Claims Court

Small claims court is the friend of most small businesses. If you find some reason to go to small claims court for traditional small business reasons, such as suing someone who won't pay a bill, you are almost certain to win if you prepare the case carefully yourself. The whole procedure is explained in the book, *Everybody's Guide to Small Claims Court*, which is available by writing to Nolo Press, Box 544, Occidental, California 95465, $5.95.

Sole Proprietorship (see Corporation and Partnership)

Unions

If you have employees, you should know about unions. The Taft-Hartley Act and the designated enforcing agency, the National Labor Relations Board (NLRB), are strongly biased toward the employer; but this is only true when the employer knows what he or she is doing.

Impending unionization can lead to much bitterness and acrimony. Many small businesses that we have known folded when they were being unionized or were sold quickly to an unsuspecting buyer. The alternative to bitterness is to know and understand the issues in advance and to know them better than your employees do, if possible. Take a course, or courses, on the subject. The few hours you spend studying the subject, and talking to the other people in the class, will be really valuable if you ever have to deal with the issue.

Once you know the legal issues of unionization, you can be quite open with your employees. If you are well informed, you can help your employees decide whether they will benefit from a union. If they can, you may encourage them to form their own union.

The one thing that employees want, but owners seldom perceive, is "security." That is what unions strive to achieve. Security takes many forms: job descriptions, cost-of-living wage increases, simple performance evaluations, clear lines of authority, grievance procedures and *seniority*. The extent to which an employer can identify with these desires for security, the more effective he or she can be in dealing with the concerns that lead to unionization.

If your employees express dissatisfaction in these areas of concern for their personal "security," then your business may face a union election. Take a course in the legal issues promptly, and don't assume that your personal charm or magnetism can dispel employee concerns.

Why Are You in Business?

This is a very important question that should be asked at regular intervals, at least twice a year, and whenever a major decision arises.

The answer to this question is the guidepost that helps you make decisions that are most relevant for your business, and will lead to the most effective practices to achieve your goals. The most important part of this exercise is to reject the answer, "I'm in business to make money." That is not the reason you are in business. Behind that quick answer is almost always the desire for respect, security, status or freedom (see Chapter 16, The Four Illusions of Money). Translate your answer directly into the desire behind it and you will find a helpful direction for your business. If you want security first, and other desires are much less important, then examine your business to see what aspects contribute to insecurity and concentrate your efforts on the elements that could provide greater security. If, for example, you have a retail toy store in a rapidly changing neighborhood, where the birth rate is declining, consider developing a mail order catalog that will give you a broader market, or visiting other countries that have rising birth rates where you might export products.

George De Woody is a leading graphic artist with a devoted following in the gay community. The demand for his work was overwhelming and his first reaction was to hire people to do the work. This did not satisfy him. Then a careful examination of why he was in business re-minded him that he wanted to be a great designer with a wide range of influence and that he didn't want to be an administrator. The solution was to hire only a few designers with whom he could work closely and to turn away less desirable business. Once he had a few designers work-ing the way he wanted them to, then he slowly let them hire and super-vise others. He also concluded that excess profits from the business should not go into expansion, but be invested in suppliers' businesses so that he could be assured of high quality support from the printers, typesetters and other people he works with.

16 · THE FOUR ILLUSIONS OF MONEY: And the Nonmoney Truths They Hide

Introduction

Our culture has come to accept greed as a positive personal value and people publicly say they "want to make a lot of money." This milieu is confusing for individuals who want to lead honest lives, as honesty and greed are countervailing forces. How do we reconcile our own needs with these conflicting paths?

The next section was written for those who know they want to lead honest lives, who know they want to serve others and yet have lingering doubts about whether neighbors with moneymaking greedy motives might be wiser.

Making a lot of money is NOT the answer to personal happiness.*

The Four Illusions of Money

Why do people work at jobs they don't like? Why is it common to hear people say their goal in life is to "make a lot of money"? These are the most frequently given answers:

"A lot of money will let me be free to do what I want."
"People with a lot of money command more respect from others."
"I need more money for my family."
"Money is necessary for security in old age."

---

* "The Four Illusions of Money" was written with the help of Andora Freeman, and appeared in the Winter 79/80 issue of *CoEvolution Quarterly*.

These statements are illusions. They are inaccurate perceptions of the world we live in.

When we look at the average graduating class of high school students, we are distressed to know that nearly all of them hold these values: they seek "a lot" of money as a lifetime goal. Less than 5 percent of these students will become wealthy. The remaining 95 percent will shape their lives around these inappropriate values.

How do *you* feel about these four statements? Read them over and see if you find them completely agreeable. For most people they are.

"A lot of money will let me be free to do what I want."

You can really feel this way when you're working at a job that you don't like, when you're unhappy with the way things are going in your life and when there is some object, experience or service you desperately want to buy.

The alternative is to deal with these feelings directly and positively. Write down the specific things you want to do with your life, the things you wish you were free to do. Describe the things you need to shape the kind of person you want to be (the experiences you need, the knowledge, skills, talents, etc.) Make sure what you write down doesn't include money itself. When you look at your list, you'll find that there is a way to accomplish all of it in your lifetime without any more money than you now have. Most things require that you actively pursue them and *learn* in the process. If you want to be a world traveler, join the crew of a sailboat or a commercial ship and be useful in a way you now know. Later you'll be skilled as a sailor and have great stories to tell about hitting sharks on the nose in the Bahamas.

What you may find from your list is that having a lot of money may allow you to achieve goals a little sooner, but the effort of going out and earning money to make something happen sooner is not worth the time, and more important, the person you may become may have lost vigor and joy.

Back in the late 1950s, a young woman who desired a doctorate degree won over $100,000 on a TV quiz show. Years later, in reflecting on the effect of the prize money, she said it made little difference in her life, although it may have accelerated obtaining her degree by a few years. She is a strong woman who knew what she wanted to do with her life. She's Dr. Joyce Brothers.

Her experience is not uncommon. People who know what they want to *do* with their lives go ahead and do it. They don't make the money first by doing something else. It often turns out that money and the possessions that go with making lots of money, are responsibilities and restrictions that inhibit freedom. The possessions unrelated to your livelihood are often amassed to help you feel better about yourself.

Check your list again and see how many possessions are among the things you want out of life. Most possessions are abundantly available. Many things can be borrowed from friends who are willing to share. That includes everything from a ski condominium to an Aston-Martin race car. With a good network of friends, nearly anything is possible. The alternative to investing your energy in making money is developing strong friendships. This means being an interesting, trustworthy and helpful person yourself.

When you are unable to locate something you need among your friends, consider renting the piece of equipment. Finding and restoring "discards" can be an alternative that saves both money and resources. Perhaps you have possessions you can trade with a friend or neighbor in exchange for something more useful. Service bartering can be an even more rewarding experience: offer to do something you're good at for a friend in exchange for a similar service. It costs no more than time and energy spent with a friend. If you have a skill, share it with others.

In writing about and examining your values, it's helpful to talk to someone who is wise. In fact, the wisdom of millions of our ancestors has been very consistent on the point of money: the goal of amassing money is traditionally called "greed" and, regardless of your motives for getting the money (freedom, charity or anything else), the results will not be what you hope for. Instead the wise teachers of tradition tell us to go ahead and do the things we want and become good at them. In that lies our freedom.

"People with a lot of money command more respect from others."

If the statement that money equals freedom is false, then so is there a fallacy behind the idea that money equals respect. Begin by making a list of the qualities you want to have, the qualities that lead others to respect you, the qualities that you want your children or your friends to have. Do words such as loyalty, honesty and generosity occur on your list? A careful examination of these qualities reveals that each of them has to do with how we conduct our daily lives and not how much money we have.

Now, make a list of the people you love and respect. Bob, Annie, Carole and David. Examine the list to see if it's ranked in the order of how much money they have. There is probably no relationship between love and the amount of money they have. The same criteria we apply to others can be applied to us. Money isn't a reason for friendship or respect.

"I need more money for my family."

Why shouldn't people be generous with their families! This seems like reasonable parental behavior. It's when people use this concept as an excuse for doing something they would rather not do that it is a fallacy. When someone works at a job that they find unpleasant, monotonous, too demanding, stressful or frustrating, and say that they do it for their family, they're talking nonsense.

Stop and ask your family what they want. Would your children rather have a Winnebago camper (which may mean the main wage earner works a lot of overtime) or would they rather have you at home to spend time with them, or go on a camping trip with ordinary sleeping bags and tents? Give your family the choice between possessions and the time and peace of mind you are diverting from them to earn it.

Another useful technique is to look at a picture of two houses—one a glamorous mansion, the other a modest home with a bicycle near the front door. Which one of the houses has a happier family? Most people would say, "I can't tell" when the question is posed this way, because we really know that money and possessions have nothing to do with happiness—given that you have enough to pay for your basic needs.

"Money is necessary for security in old age."

Michael is blessed with a father who is a living contradiction of this statement. When he was sixty-five, his father retired from teaching anthropology and social sciences with a modest pension and social security income of $300 a month. He sold his home and all his belongings, including a lifetime collection of tools and books (this bought almost no revenue). He bought a van in England and proceeded to drive east with his wife. He got teaching jobs along the way and stopped anyplace he found interesting.

Driving as far east as they could go, they ended up in Malaysia, where they bought part of a South China Sea island near Singapore for $2,000. They now live part time on their island with a sandy beach, coconut trees, fresh fish and lots of Malaysian and Chinese friends. They live on less than $100 a month, and save the rest for numerous trips they take to all parts of the world, including back to the U.S. One of the most surprising benefits is that they regularly see many of their old friends from all over the world. Everyone wants to visit their tropical paradise for a vacation. With Singapore nearby, they have all the comforts of a major international city with its cuisine, culture and excitement.

From the Grey Panthers to people in retirement villages, those who are happy in their old age are people that have the qualities of being friendly and flexible and who know friendship is more powerful than money. With friends and family, especially those of all ages, you can solve most of the problems that arise, whether it's tax increases, inflation or legal hassles—problems that other people can't handle because times have changed and their lifetime experiences and contacts are inappropriate. Friends also provide vitality, emotional support and new friends— which is especially valuable after age seventy-five when one out of ten old friends die each year.

Flexibility in attitude is also essential when your body becomes less reliable. We all know old people who say, "Close the window, the draft is terrible," "I can't sleep in that bed, it's too soft" and "I don't like to be around those kinds of people." What a contrast to Pete Albini, a wonderful Italian farmer in his early seventies and a close friend of Rasberry. When some minor disaster strikes him, Pete peers straight ahead, lifts up his cap, scratches his head and says something like "These things just happen" and goes on with whatever needs to be done. His contentment and happiness stem from his commitment to help his friends and neighbors. If your car gets stuck or your calf is sick or your relationship is skittery, you can share a cup of coffee at Pete's kitchen table and he will help you or will find someone who can. You can't leave his house without a carton of eggs, some fresh milk or a pound of butter. Pete has friends of all ages who vie for the privilege of helping him when they can. Pete may not have a lot of money but he's a wealthy man, secure in his later years.

We have worked with many older people who had lots of money. In cases where the husband has earned the money, we frequently find that the husband is confident and secure, but the wife is anxious and often hysterical. He has earned the money in the first place, and knows he could do it again, even in his old age; the woman has no such experience and dreads the day when her husband will die and she has to face the world alone. No amount of money that we have seen can calm this kind of fear.

How do you prepare for old age? How do you prepare for inflations, wars and depressions of the future? By being the kind of person other people want to be around: competent, helpful, flexible, curious, generous and experienced in dealing with the world.

Summary

You can accomplish what you want from life by pursuing your interests and passions. Rather than seeking possessions, develop strong friendships and become an interesting person. Give your family and friends the gift of yourself and they will treasure you far more than material objects. You can have a great deal of freedom and respect during your life and security in your old age. However, if you are a loner, rather selfish, with narrow interests, then making a lot of money may be your only way to make it through life.

17 · FOUR HONEST MEN WHO CHANGED BUSINESS

We have selected four men whose lives are examples of honesty in business and who made singularly important contributions to American business. The first, A. P. Giannini, founded and built the Bank of America, which grew to be the largest bank in the world, and pioneered the areas of consumer loans and branch banking. William Cooper Procter headed Procter & Gamble, a modern-day giant that is still a leading innovator in consumer products, and established the first profit-sharing plan in a sizable U.S. company, guaranteed employees forty-eight weeks of work in each year and initiated the five-and-a-half-day work week. James Cash Penney created the largest and most unusual chain of dry goods stores in his day and initiated the concept of the self-renewing organization through store partnerships. Theodore Vail is the father of American Telephone and Telegraph and was the leading pioneer in creating effective corporate scientific research at the Bell Laboratories. Through his leadership at Bell Telephone, he built a utility whose large size and efficiency gave the United States a technological advantage for fifty years.

These men were the epitome of honesty in business. Integrity was their hallmark and their persistence in carrying their own honesty and openness into business helped them to see and implement strategies that others missed. Their business astuteness would have allowed each of them to readily succeed in business, but it was their honesty that led them to make major contributions to, and innovations in, the marketplace.

Amadeo Peter Giannini (1870–1949)

A.P., to everyone who knew him, was a vegetable trader from his early teens until he retired at thirty-one with a sizable fortune and partnership income from the largest produce commission firm in the San Francisco Bay Area. The son of an immigrant, his close friends and his community were Italian teamsters, stevedores, farmers and vegetable merchants. A.P. was remembered by friends from this early period as rough, friendly, a tireless worker and always a "square shooter."

The youthful retired merchant was invited to serve on the board of Columbus Savings and Loan, a local association that served Italian fishermen in San Francisco's North Beach. He was dismayed to find the board position being used by other members for their personal gain, and the board's general disinterest in the financial needs of his small-business peers. A.P.'s interest was in helping his friends and fellow immigrant Italians. "I don't want to be rich . . . no man actually ever owns a fortune . . . it owns him."

In 1904, with his friends, he started the Bank of Italy across the street from the Columbus Savings and Loan, to help the "little man who needed a little money." Banking at the turn of the century was a top hat, silk-shirt business, where the minimum opening deposit for a checking account was $5,000. In contrast, A.P. welcomed everyone to his new bank, encouraged small opening deposits and was the first banker to use the ideas of Robert Morris (the Virginian who developed the Morris Plan), by making personal loans to business people repayable in installments.

During the earthquake and fire of 1906 he personally removed the gold from his bank before it was destroyed, and as soon as the fire was out, opened a storefront branch office that cashed checks for every bank's customers. This act ultimately gained him a respected reputation in many business circles. A.P. pioneered branch banking, seeking convenient bank locations for his customers. As his bank grew he visited each branch often, talking with tellers, bookkeepers and new employees, reminding them that his "door was always open." The Bank of Italy grew rapidly; when it had over one hundred branches it bought a small, sixteen-year-old bank called the Bank of America and took on the small bank's name. Today it is the largest bank in the world.

Before A.P. retired again in the 1930s, he encouraged more liberal home loans—which at the time required 50 percent cash deposit and were amortized over fifteen years—and built a headquarters building where every member of the bank's top management worked in one large room. He felt that such openness among top executives discouraged political infighting and promoted the confidence of fellow employees.

A.P. was never a large shareholder in the Bank of America and gave away much of his money. "Hell, why should a man pile up a lot of god-damned money for somebody else to spend after he's gone?" He returned to banking in 1938 after waging a two-year proxy battle to regain control of his bank. He campaigned throughout California, personally visiting small shareholders, getting their support for his goal of returning the bank to the policies of helping the "little man" whom he felt was being ignored by the bank in his absence.

William Cooper Procter (1862–1934)

Procter & Gamble was founded in Cincinnati on an ethical tradition and a strict policy of giving consistent quality and honest weight to its customers. The guiding philosophy of the manufacturers of Crisco and Ivory soap was an "honest return for an honest dollar." The admission of Ivory soap's impurity became an asset: "99 44/100 percent pure" won the hearts of Americans. William Cooper joined Procter & Gamble in 1883 and rose up through the ranks. The company was headed by his father and had been founded by his grandfather, William Procter, and an associate, James Gamble.

Procter accepted a trust from his father and apprenticed himself to learn all the details of Procter & Gamble that only hands-on experience could give him. Those early years spent in overalls gave him a proximity with, and a natural understanding of the worker which greatly influenced his policy making during his fifty-two years of active service.

William Cooper lived during the time when manufacturing was making the transition to large-scale, mechanized production. Strikes were epidemic as employers and workers were assumed to be natural enemies. Factory workers were placated during strikes and treated as servants the rest of the time. Procter & Gamble itself had a 50 percent labor turnover.

Procter realized that the spirit and well-being of his workers was at the heart of production success. He set about creating good will between management and labor by providing more equitable treatment of labor. He initiated the radical notion of the Saturday half-day holiday without loss of pay. This was the first five-and-a-half-day work week offered by an American industrial concern. In 1915, at a time when any employment benefits were rare, he offered his workers pension plans and sickness and death benefits. He had pioneered a profit-sharing plan as early as 1887. It was one of the first experiments of its kind, making the employee a partner and enabling him or her to work *with*, instead of *for*, the company.

Seasonal variation in the production schedule caused many layoffs at Procter & Gamble. This layoff problem continually threatened the job security that was the workers' most important concern. Procter reasoned that a full employment plan would ease the minds of his employees and attract the steady kind of worker he wanted. In 1923, he caused a sensation in the industrial world by devising a guaranteed full employment plan. This radical departure meant a complete reorientation of the entire selling department, equalizing distribution over the year by allowing small retail stores to order directly from the company instead of having to go through a few large middle-jobbers.

Procter and his wife had no children, so civic concerns and the business of Procter & Gamble occupied most of his time. Procter & Gamble was known for its support of the war effort, so it was not surprising that Procter, a quiet man of military bearing who saw the point of business in human values, wrote his niece, "Procter & Gamble are very fortunate and have enough raw material to last them a year and could make a great deal of money out of their position, but I am going to try not to do so. We are practically not going to advance prices at all, but base our selling prices upon our cost prices of our raw materials and not upon their present value which I think is about $8,000,000.00 more than what they cost. I don't want to make any money out of the war, and I don't want the Company to do so. I am afraid we will have trouble holding our prices down as our orders will be more than we can fill, but I have already told the Procter & Gamble office to notify our trade that we would regulate our shipments as we thought fair and not on the basis of what a man had ordered."

James Cash Penney (1875–1971)

James Cash Penney grew up on a Missouri farm during the late 1800s. His father was a Baptist lay preacher who instilled in his son the importance of honesty and self-reliance; of fairness and applying the golden rule philosophy to everyday living. His father told him "Don't ever let me see a son of mine take advantage of others for his own benefit. When I'm gone, Jim, if people passing my grave can say, 'Here lies all that is mortal of an honest man,' I couldn't ask for anything better. It's the finest thing a man can have remembered about him."

The Penney Dry Goods Stores were built on the golden rule premise of "Do unto others as you would be done by," and Penney was able to fashion an incredibly successful business structure into which he could pour his considerable passion to serve others. J. C. wanted to provide the average person with quality goods at fair prices and his prices were very low as compared to others. Opening his first stores in small country towns with populations of a thousand to three thousand people, he was able to cater to the basic needs of rural America.

When Penney went on buying trips he carted swatches of fabric samples back to his hotel room washing them by hand to see that they didn't shrink or run and to insure his customers of first-quality goods. He avoided expensive locations, had no fancy fixtures and in every way tried to save his customers money. Contrary to the custom of the day, he piled merchandise on tables where customers could feel the goods themselves. He also established one price for all. If customers were dissatisfied they could return merchandise for full credit. These practices seem common now but were revolutionary in 1910.

The key to the success of the Penney stores were the men who managed them. In the early years each manager was personally known by Penney to be extremely honest and to adhere to the spirit of the golden rule, insuring a fair deal to his fellow workers and to customers.

The Penney store was an important part of its community and would extend credit in times of hardship. So trusted were these shopkeepers that lumberjacks would leave six months' pay for safekeeping with a Penney manager they had never seen before but whom they trusted merely because of the store's reputation. This community concern exists to this day and the company's behavior a few years ago during the Alaskan earthquake of 1964 is a good example. Property damage ran into the hundreds of millions and the new Penney store in Alaska was completely destroyed. Concerned that the citizens of Anchorage would not be able to buy necessities, Penney's announced a moratorium on payments due from their customers, many of whom had lost their homes and all their belongings. Three temporary stores were opened and all employees were kept on the payroll.

At a time when a community particularly needed a vote of confidence Penney's was able to respond. The result was that customers offered to figure out with the store the status of their accounts and paid for merchandise Penney's didn't even know they were owed. Penney's bad debt loss was negligible.

Penney's stores had such an impact on the public that sometimes customers would petition the firm to locate in their town!

The strength of J. C. Penney's company lay in the unique partnership arrangement Penney and his early associates devised to insure the success of their chain of dry goods stores. The plan was simple and equitable: a manager who could save enough capital could buy a one-third ownership in a new chain store. Thus his success would be directly linked with the success of the store and one-third of the profits would be his. He in turn would train his head clerk to become a Penney manager and consequently the links would grow. Penney stores thus became a self-renewing organization. In 1927, Penney fully incorporated and from that point on managers were given stock in the company chain, making them dependent on the profits of their particular store for success.

Penney, the "man with a thousand partners," in speaking of his own life said, "Were I to commence again . . . giving men an opportunity to share in what they help to create would remain one of my cardinal principles."

Theodore N. Vail (1845–1920)

Theodore N. Vail was a large, gregarious man whose imprint on American business is major. He ran the telephone company at two crucial junctures in its development, and is credited with having created the largest nongovernmental phone company in the world at a time when most phone systems were government agencies.

Vail's experience before age thirty-three was with the postal service. By twenty-nine, he had worked his way up to Assistant General Superintendent of Railway Postal Service, where he inaugurated the first "Fast Mail" service. These express mail trains went nonstop from New York to Chicago in 26.5 hours, the fastest long-distance run made by any railway train up to that time. The service was rapidly expanded to other cities, and each railroad car was distinctively painted white and named after a governor, whose name was lettered on the side in gold.

Vail's administrative experience and vision were applied for nine years to the creation of the Bell Telephone Company where he worked as a trustee for Alexander G. Bell's original patents. Before he retired he started the American Telephone and Telegraph Co., as a long-distance system to connect the many growing independent phone exchanges.

Vail spent twenty years in retirement, much of it on a farm in Vermont, living on a few successful investments. He invested in many scientifically based businesses and supported any business he felt would revolutionize industry. His home was open to anyone as he had an almost childlike trust in others. "I would rather get cheated now and then than distrust anybody," was his personal investment policy. He spent considerable time in South America, helping build power plants and street railways in Argentina.

In 1907, at age sixty-two, Vail returned to the telephone company after the death of his wife of forty-nine years and their only son. These events seem to have transformed him. He brought new vigor with him to serve people to the phone industry, and at this time made the major contributions for which he is most famous. He foresaw the need for an effective telephone network to expand the telephone system, brought about by cooperation between the competing independent phone companies. To this end, he raised funds for his company by selling public stock to small investors on a massive and innovative scale. He was always frank with the public. His first annual report was opposed by many of his directors. He argued, "We will lay our cards on the table; there is never anything to be gained by concealment." His openness with shareholders and the public became the model of the best in public relations. His guideline was, "Take the public into your confidence and you win the confidence of the public." With the funds raised from shareholders, he proceeded to buy as many small phone companies as were willing to sell, at virtually any price asked; for those remaining, he offered cooperation with contractual agreements to use AT&T long-distance lines. His object was, "One policy, one system, and universal service," a pioneering concept before the monopoly aspects of the phone industry became obvious. To avoid government ownership, he encouraged and, in some cases, helped establish regulatory bodies to set telephone rates.

During the First World War, Vail fought congressional efforts to nationalize the phone company, but he lost his fight in 1918. After the defeat, he traveled to Washington, D.C., to personally hand over his company and give his support to the Postmaster General. He was told to go back to New York and to continue running the company; after the war it would be returned to its owners.

Vail established Western Electric as the manufacturing arm of the Bell system, and created the research program that became the famous Bell Laboratories. The Bell Laboratories' research was first focused on the vacuum tubes and relays that Vail understood to be vital to the growth of the phone network. Without automation, the switchboard and labor demand would grow faster than the number of new phones; the only hope was electronic research. In addition to this technology, which was developed and introduced rapidly, the extremely important Bell Labs were to introduce television, computers, transistors and lasers.

Vail was noted for his candor and honesty, and was a man of great vision. Everything he touched expanded to large proportions. In a little more than forty years, he formed the largest, most efficient telephone system in the world. When Vail was seventy, he gave away his immense farm to the state of Vermont to be used by the agricultural schools for boys and girls, which he had founded some years before, reserving the right to live there until his death.

APPENDIX

A. History of Business

The history of business extends back more than eight thousand years. Surprisingly, most of the common elements of today's business were familiar to business people long ago.

The best description of business practices among ancient traders comes from Malcolm Margolin's *The Ohlone Way* (Heyday Books, Box 9145, Berkeley, CA 94709, $4.95.). Margolin's description of traders visiting a tribe of Ohlone people in Northern California is actually taken from anthropological records and interviews with surviving Indians. The Ohlone were a people who lived a relaxed life, peacefully thriving on abundant food that they hunted and gathered. They survived until the end of the nineteenth century. Their business practices and daily lives were very much like those of peoples the world over before agriculture began to change the social structure thousands of years ago. Even as cities grew to protect and support agriculture, traders continued to flourish, trading over long distances between cities and towns. Many of the traders' methods were carried over to city business practices.

Margolin begins his description of traders very slowly, setting the mood that accurately portrays the pace of our ancestors and warrants respect.

For three days everyone in the village has moved slowly, languidly—ever since the men returned from the off-shore islands, their boats filled with cormorant eggs. For three days everyone has feasted on the strong, fishy tasting eggs. It is late morning now, and most of the villagers are napping in the shade, except for one old woman.

She is much older than anyone else in the village—well over a hundred years old—and she has been blind for so long that most of the villagers do not remember the time when she was sighted. Her own children are long dead and even her grandchildren, those who are still alive, are now old men and women. She is cared for by great-grandchildren and great-great-grandchildren for whom she is a relic of an ancient past well beyond the memory of anyone else in the tribelet, a past which will be forever lost to tribal knowledge when she dies. She has eaten very little in recent years, and her mind has become somewhat addled. Most of the time she sleeps; but curiously, now that nearly everyone else in the village is sleeping she is wide awake, sitting before her house in the full sun, singing an old-time song:

> He is beating your wife now.
> It is Pelican who is beating her.

This song was first sung long ago in Sacred Time to Fog, who was thereby told to rush back home because Pelican was assaulting his wife. Now it is sung as a powerful charm, one that can bring a man home from far away. Although it has been many years since there was any man for her to draw homewards, the old woman sings it over and over again in a cracked, wavering voice. There is no other sound in the village, and the few people who are not napping listen idly. They listen and they drowse, for even the children are full of cormorant eggs. And that morning—the first really hot day of spring—it seems that nothing will ever rouse them.

But suddenly the village does come astir. A runner is seen heading toward the village from the north. As he approaches, the chief's speaker comes out to greet him and escorts him to the chief's house. The runner, who is well known in the village—he is a member of the tribelet immediately to the north—delivers his message. A group of traders, great men, very great men, are seeking the chief's permission to visit the village. The chief ponders for a moment and then gives the runner a carved "invitation stick" to hand to the traders. He also gives the runner a string of beads as payment for having delivered the message.

As soon as the runner departs the chief rouses his wives and instructs them to prepare a feast. The other people of the village mill about, looking toward the north, eager to catch the first glimpse of the traders. Time passes slowly.

"I see them, I see them," declares a young hunter who has sharper eyes than the others. "They are heading this way."

"Perhaps they are antelopes," suggests another tactfully. "Antelopes sometimes look like people from a great distance."

"No, they are men. I see them. There are five men. They all have carrying nets. Carrying nets," he adds, squinting his eyes. Then, filled with a sense of his own importance, he continues his description, adopting the repetitive, rhythmic speaking style of the village's great orators. "They are moving slowly. Look how slowly they move. Their carrying nets are heavy, heavy with many things. Look, their carrying nets are heavy. They are moving slowly and their carrying nets are heavy, heavy with many things. They are moving slowly. They are moving this way. They are moving slowly."

The travelers draw closer to the village; soon everyone can see that indeed there are five men and that their carrying nets are bulging with goods. What's more, to judge from their ornaments and markings, these are strangers from a considerable distance. They are people the villagers have never seen before.

The chief's three wives redouble their efforts to prepare the food. The wives are all daughters of chiefs—they come from the tribelets to the north, south, and east—and they are accustomed to entertaining important visitors. The other women of the village, however, withdraw into their houses, pulling their children after them and covering the entranceways with tule mats. Then, settling themselves on the floors of their houses, they peek through the mats to catch a glimpse of the strangers.

Men of ordinary families also withdraw and cluster around the sweathouse. Only the prominent men of the village remain visible. They have painted their bodies and tucked their most splendid feathers into their hairnets. The chief moves nervously among them, preparing them for the arrival of the strangers. "They are strangers," he says. "We do not know who they are. We do not know where they come from. We must see if they know how to behave. Their nets are heavy." In this way the chief goes among the people: and while his words urge them toward moderation, his manner excites them still further.

At last the five strangers reach the outskirts of the village. Here they pause and speak loudly, ostensibly to each other, but really to let the sound of their voices carry into the village. They speak in a foreign language. Within the houses the women giggle at the sound of the words—and for many months after the visit they will imitate the accents of the strangers, making each other laugh even at the memory of it.

Now, out of the midst of the prominent men, the chief's speaker steps toward the strangers. He stands before them and gives them a long speech of welcome. They have come from far away. They look tired. They have arrived among good people. The chief's wives are preparing a feast. It will be good to stop, it will be good to rest. "After all," he says, his voice full of innuendo, "your carrying nets are very heavy."

The innuendo is, of course, totally lost on the strangers, since they have understood nothing of the long speech. Nevertheless, they feel a great sense of relief at the sound of his voice. They are happy to know that they have entered a proper village. It puts their minds at ease for the first time since mid-afternoon when they met a man (they would long remember him!) who lived alone in the woods—a man who lived completely alone, without relatives or friends to protect and help him. The man had been rude to them, insisting that they trade with him. When they refused, he made threatening gestures. The strangers pushed past him, clutching tightly to their invitation stick, worrying that they had traveled beyond the land of proper people. Perhaps this was not a man at all, they thought, but a spirit who would do them harm. But now, as they listen to the words of the chief's speaker, they know for certain that they are among a good people and they are much relieved.

When the speaker finishes, the oldest of the five strangers steps forward. He is a rugged looking, heavy-set man. Tattoos cover his forearms and shins, and he has an ornamental eagle-down rope slung around his shoulders. He explains (using many gestures) that his party has been traveling for two days, and that their village lies far to the north. He talks about his people and the purpose of his journey. He talks at length. His speech may be quite elegant, but of course the village speaker understands none of it. But by watching the man's gestures carefully, by hearing the tones of repetition and the sonorous quality of his voice, he knows at once that this is a person of high birth, and he beckons the strangers to follow him to the chief's dwelling.

The chief has seated himself near the entrance of his house, and he now presents a most imposing figure. He has painted his body so that one half is black, the other half a silvery white. He has fastened his hair on top of his head with a wooden four-pronged "comb." He is wearing long wooden ear plugs and a bone nose plug decorated with delicate incisions. Over his shoulders he has slung a cape of feathers—many different, brightly colored feathers woven into strking patterns that form an absolutely resplendent garment.

As the strangers come into his presence, his wives put five fresh tule mats on the ground for them to sit on, and straightway they bring the guests seed cakes, acorn bread, and a great heap of cormorant eggs. It has begun to grow dark and a fire is lit. The wives bring still more food: fish, elk meat, roots, and all kinds of delicacies.

The guests study the chief closely. They do not know this village and its customs, and they are afraid of doing something wrong—something that will insult the chief, perhaps enrage him. The chief is aware of the strangers' predicament, and despite three days of gorging himself he eats heartily. The guests follow his example. The chief feels proud: to be able to prepare such a feast on the spur of the moment is a very great accomplishment.

After the meal the chief begins to talk. For him conversation with the strangers is no problem. He speaks the languages of all the surrounding people, and while he is not familiar with the native language of the

traders he discovers that they have in common the language of an inter-
vening people. As he speaks, the chief uses an aristocratic accent and in
fact an aristocratic vocabulary and grammar that differ noticeably from
the more common people's language. The head trader responds in kind,
showing (as if there were any doubt) that he also comes from a noble and
well-connected family.

After much polite and round-about conversation the chief phrases the
big question. "Do you have anything to trade?" he asks, pointing to the
bulging carrying nets to assure himself that his meaning will not be lost.

The leader of the group nods. Without further ado he pulls a large
skin out of his carrying net and opens it up to display a wide variety of
obsidian arrowheads, axe heads, drill bits, and knife blades. The chief can
scarcely believe his eyes. He has seen obsidian before, certainly. Bits and
pieces of it have come his way, some from the Sierras, some from Glass
Mountain quarry in Wappo territory. But never in his life has he seen
such a vast quantity of it together in one place. He gazes over the arrowheads and knife blades. He notices how their chipped facets reflect the
fire. By shifting his head he finds that he can catch the image of the fire
itself burning deep inside the axe head.

"All of it?" he asks, waving his hand over the whole skin.

"All of it," agrees the stranger.

The chief goes into his house and empties a pile of shell money out of
a basket—strands of clamshell disks, tiny, even, and well-polished, strung
on fine strong string. He measures out several lengths of money. Then,
thinking about the obsidian, he measures out still more. As he is about to
leave the house, he hesitates for a moment, and grabs still another long
strand. After all, such an extraordinary wealth of obsidian!

The chief lays the pile of money beads before the stranger. The
stranger looks them over and notices that they are well made and even.
He examines one strand closely and places it against the measuring marks
tattooed on his arm. Roughly judging the value of the entire pile, without
counting or measuring any further, he smiles his agreement at the chief.
The trade is accomplished.

The chief is gratified. He is delighted not only with the obsidian, but
also with the fine manners of the strangers. Here is a man who does not
count his beads too closely, who does not stoop to bickering and bargaining. The chief feels certain that he is in the presence of an extraordinary
man, a man of good birth, and he longs to get to know him better.

"Do you have anything else to trade?" asks the chief. Almost at once
the stranger pulls out something even more wonderful than the obsidian.
At first the chief can scarcely understand what the stranger is holding before him. They are shells, yes, a string of shells, but shells that he has
never seen before in his whole life. (These would have been dentalia

shells all the way from Vancouver Island in Canada.) The chief is struck speechless. Here is something new, something with colors and a shape he has never seen before—in fact, something he has never even conceived of before.

As the chief takes the shells in his hand, turning them over and over as if to search out their mystery, he realizes that the stranger is staring at him. This is indeed a powerful man, a man full of magic, and the chief knows that his own liberality is now being tested to the utmost. He goes immediately into his house, and when he returns he lays before the stranger the most valuable thing he has: a big chunk of cinnabar ore that he himself has only recently received in trade. (The cinnabar, highly valued as a pigment, would have come from the "New Almaden" mines near present-day San Jose.)

The stranger is very pleased with the cinnabar. Later, he will remove a chunk for his own use and work the rest into standard-sized trading balls. When he returns home he will trade these to the people north of him who will in turn trade them still further north, until eventually pieces of the cinnabar might even reach the borders of the Columbia River.

The four men who have accompanied the stranger now take their own carrying nets and circulate among the other prominent men of the village, leaving the chief and the head trader alone. The wives offer them more food. The chief presents the stranger with an especially valuable gift basket filled with salt. As they sit together they no longer feel quite so strange in each other's company. They would very much like to see each other again, perhaps every year. They would like to become "favored trading partners," each saving his most special trade goods for the other. To have such a man as a "favored trading partner" would be fully as valuable as the obsidian or the dentalia, reflects the chief as he brings out a pipe and offers the stranger some tobacco. . . .

The Ohlones loved to trade, as did all California Indians. Extensive networks of trails and trade routes criss-crossed the entire state, north and south, east and west—trails that extended through Oregon and the Pacific Northwest, trails that crossed the Central Valley to the Sierras and beyond to the Great Basin. The California Indians viewed trading as an ancient, almost permanent part of their world. And with justification; a string of coastal shell beads some 9,000 years old has been found in a cave in Nevada, evidence of a long, long history of intertribal trade.

Trading was, of course, largely a matter of business: but since it was Ohlone business, it was governed not so much by the profit motive, but rather by the ethic of sharing and the overruling virtue of generosity. A trader laid out his goods and his opposite made an offer. The offer was almost always accepted: in fact, it was considered rude to haggle. If the offer was too miserly, the person who made it would quickly gain a bad reputation, and other people would refuse to trade with him. In these tiny communities, where nothing was forgotten, no one wanted a bad reputation, and both parties strove to be as generous as possible. They tried to treat each other as "family" rather than competitors, to deepen their ties and perhaps to become "favored trading partners."

Generosity, which regulated individual behavior, also governed political relationships between different groups. Not only were individuals expected to be generous, but tribelets were expected to be generous as well. A group which lived along a rich salmon creek did not, for example, hoard its catch, but shared it with others. Visitors passing through were always given gifts of salmon, and in years of plenty the salmon-rich tribelet entertained its neighbors with lavish salmon feasts. The other tribelets, in turn, reciprocated with gifts of shellfish, seeds, game, skins, nuts, or precious minerals. Also, between salmon runs or in years when the salmon catch was low, the salmon-fishing tribelet would visit its neighbors, fully expecting to be feasted and entertained.

Similarly, if a tribelet had a valuable oyster bed, mine, quarry, asphaltum seep, or other resource on its territory, it would generally let other groups pass through to use it. Everyone expected this; if one tribelet tried to deny others entry, war might even result. Visiting tribelets did not take entry for granted, however, but were expected to ask for proper permission and bring proper gifts.

Thus the Ohlones were not forty independent, isolated tribelets jealously guarding their frontiers. Rather, each tribelet was involved in a network of feasting, trading, and gift-giving. Certain villages within the Ohlone world took on the role of ceremonial and trade centers, attracting people from miles around. Each triblet was linked to its neighbors by the most intimate and complex bonds of marriage and traditional collecting rights in nearby territories. Throughout the year different groups tried to treat their neighbors well—to entertain them, be generous, and cooperate with them—and in turn each group expected to be treated well by its neighbors. In fact the sharing of food and other resources was so successful and reliable that it was one of the major reasons why famine was totally unknown in Central California.

Yet while cooperation between the tribelets was extremely important, it did not work easily or perfectly. The tribelets acted generously toward each other, but at the same time they usually regarded each other with a constant, gnawing irritability. Hatreds continually flared up. A slight became a grudge, and in these small tribelets grudges were nurtured until they became feuds. One could never be thoroughly at ease with foreigners. They spoke in peculiar ways and cooked their food differently. Their shamans were forever poisoning one's daughters or changing into bears to inflict disease and death upon one's relatives. When the insults and magic became totally intolerable, skirmishes, even warfare, would occasionally break out.

Thus the relationship between different tribelets was marked by the strongest of attractions and at the same time the strongest of repulsions. The people were generous and hospitable, yet underneath they often seethed with suspicions. Their dislike of each other kept the Ohlones apart: forty or so independent tribelets, speaking eight to twelve different languages. Yet their intimate family, trading, and other economic ties kept their dislike in check. In this way the Ohlones had achieved a relationship that served to keep the tribelets together—but not too together; apart— but not too apart. In fact (if one were to ask an Ohlone) they had achieved a relationship between the tribelets that served to keep things pretty much as they had been since the beginning of time.

This next description is of a city whose business practices were very similar to ours today.

Recent excavations in Syria have unearthed a city called Ebla which thrived for several centuries beginning more than four thousand years ago. In the ruins of Ebla were found more than ten thousand inscribed clay tablets which include much information about business, language and history. The following description is taken from published material about Ebla. The names used were common names in Ebla and are translations from the Semitic language of the period. These names predate the recorded biblical personages by several centuries.

We are in Ebla, a prosperous commercial city of twenty thousand people, and a key link in a thriving trading network. The Mediterranean is fifty miles to the west of us, the Euphrates River is sixty miles to the east. South by three hundred miles are the trading ports of Gaza and Jaffa, and the flourishing cities of Sodom, Gomorrah and Jerusalem.

Historically, Ebla is an early city. The growth of cities dates back only a couple of thousand years before it. The oldest written records, on clay tablets, have only been around for about five hundred years.

In five hundred to eight hundred more years, a small trading tribe, variously called Israelites, Hebrews and Jews, would grow rapidly, and survive to the present day. Two thousand years after the period described, a man named Jesus of Nazareth was to organize a following that would, among other things, make his birthday one of the first worldwide measures of time.

Today, in this account, we stop at a shop on the market plaza to describe what business is like in Ebla. The shop, 15 feet by 20 feet, is owned by Abraham and Michael, two brothers in their mid-forties who have formed a partnership. We join them for hot mint cola tea served on small benches at the entrance to the shop. Abraham and Michael sell bronze and brass teapots and serving platters, inlaid wooden stools, benches and treasure boxes, and woolen carpets.

The bronze and brass pieces come mostly from Babylon, brought by traveling caravans. Some of the inlaid wooden pieces come from Aleppo. The rest are made of teak and olive wood, and have been constructed in Ebla. The carpets are bought on trips to the neighboring towns of Emar and Carchemish, about sixty miles distant.

Abraham does most of the buying, paying for goods in silver and gold granules, measured out in shekels on a large balance scale. One shekel of silver is the price of a garment-size piece of cotton cloth, one of Ebla's most renowned products. Six shekels of silver equal one of gold. Abraham also deals with Isaiah, Saul, Israel and Malik of Canaan, the carpenters who make the inlaid wood products, and Esther, the owner of the shop building. Isaiah and Saul do most of the carpentry work on the wood that Abraham provides for them. As the work is finished, Abraham negotiates a price for the work based on quality and style. Careful bargaining results in a payment that is usually equal to 15 percent of the final sale price. The price varies with the amount of business that Abraham and Michael have been doing for the past month, and the finances of Isaiah and Saul. Saul often gets less because he gets drunk occasionally, gambles and has no children. Israel and Malik of Canaan do the inlay work. Israel is paid the same way that Isaiah and Saul are. Malik was brought from Canaan because of his unusual tradition. He lives in a house near the Gate of Sipish (the Sun God), one of the four gates to the city, with his wife and three children. Abraham and Michael own the house, and regularly bring Malik barley, oats, honey, goat's milk and corn. In addition, they give him 2 silver shekels weekly as savings for his return to Canaan, and as supplementary spending money. The wood Abraham provides his workers is usually olive or teak. The teak comes from Indian traders, but the olive comes from Ugarit. Abraham pays for this by special arrangement, as the Ugarites are very cautious people. He gives 20 shekels of silver to Abraham of Ur,* a reliable trader who gets the best buy he can for olive wood in Ugarit. The family who sells the wood to Abraham of Ur gives him a clay ball with a seal on the outside to return to Abraham, the merchant of Ebla. When it is opened in Ebla, the price of the wood

---

* The Ebla excavations have uncovered the existence of a small town in northern Syria, known as "Ur," which is likely to be the actual home of Abraham the Patriarch, rather than Ur of the Chaldees, far to the southeast in Mesopotamia.

and the number of pieces is recorded on the inside. Abraham of Ur is paid 25 percent for his labor.

Abraham's toughest assignment is dealing with Esther, who inherited the shop from her great-grandfather, who built the store with a house above it after the city of Ebla was sacked in a war with Akkad, three hundred and fifty miles to the southeast. Negotiations with Esther take many hours, and are held every month at the new moon. Esther wants 10 percent of all the store earns. Abraham tells Esther, one by one, each of the monthly sales (e.g.: Miriam, wife of Saul, paid 2 shekels for a 3 x 3 rug). Esther argues and disputes, offering rumors and market gossip she has heard as counterevidence. Only once have they gone to court to settle their differences. It was over a large chest that was returned many months after it was sold. Esther wouldn't give back 10 percent of the rental price to Abraham. The king, who was Irkab-Damu at the time, agreed with Abraham and ordered repayment. Kings, who are elected to a seven-year term in office by all Eblites, have absolute power.

Michael handles the store and sales along with his two sons and two daughters, who run errands, bringing water, baklava and fresh flowers. The store opens about three hours before noon every day except holidays, closes for two hours at noon, and opens again for five hours in the afternoon. Flags, banners and a Persian carpet are put in front of the store every day. Serious customers are offered tea and pastries while they negotiate. Michael deals with local politics, pays the tribute (taxes of twelve gubars, equivalent to six bushels, of barley, or its equivalent, per year) and special levies, donates to needy families and to special subscriptions. He also lends money, on occasion, to old friends and relatives, at 20 percent interest, repayable annually. He also arranges the banquets and gifts that are part of the fare for regular customers and powerful people. At night, Michael leaves the store with his oldest son, who sleeps there to protect the valuable inventory.

Most of the elements of business that exist today can be found in the descriptions of the Ohlone people and the residents of Ebla. The two major exceptions are the corporation and fixed retail prices, innovations that are more recent. Corporations are legal entities based on a structural concept of perpetual life, resembling churches and governments in their legal form, and in this way differ from the traditional partnership form of business. They appear to have evolved in the East, in China, during the twelfth century, and in the West out of Royal Charters giving exclusive trading rights to English and Dutch traders during the seventeenth century colonization. The corporation came into common use in business at the beginning of the nineteenth century. Fixed prices, publicly marked on goods, gained acceptance as an effective sales technique about 125 years ago.

B. Honest Business in the Broader Context

Three questions are frequently raised about honest business. How big can honest business get? Are there any things about honest business that can be applied to existing corporations? What are the implications of honest business in the world market?

The answer to all three questions comes from an examination of the concept of what a large business is. To examine this concept, let's compare Safeway, a well-run supermarket chain with several thousand stores, to a comparable number of similar-sized supermarkets that are independent. In both Safeway and the independents, there are thousands of people who go to work each day, and do very similar work: delivering, cleaning and selling food. The difference is that Safeway has more individuals involved, full time, in specialized business functions such as hiring of personnel, supervising security, finding new locations and dealing with the financial community. These specialized functions are handled differently by independent stores. For the independent, small segments of the manager's daily time is dedicated to these functions.

What is the difference between a large company and the cluster of businesses? The difference is the communications mechanism of the two systems, which determines how well the people involved work together. This, in turn, determines how large the single business can grow.

At Safeway, the communication occurs through internal memoranda, instructions passed through the chain of command, existing policies and traditions of doing business, extensive friendship networks of people who regularly mingle because they have the commonalty of a paycheck coming from Safeway, and informal personal networks—grapevines. The independent grocers have similar mechanisms, but they lack the memoranda process and chain of command instructions. Instead, they rely on trade journals, market price information and gossip from sales people, bankers and brokers.

Which of the two systems delivers food at the lowest price, offers the best quality and service to its customers and provides the most desirable working conditions for the people involved? Both seem equal right now. Safeway is not growing much anymore; it is approaching its size limit. Safeway does not offer better food at lower prices than an independent store because its communication is not superior.

It is common to assume that production processes determine the size of a business. For example, the assumption is that a large company is necessary to manufacture steel, aluminum, tanker ships, etc. In fact, economists are finding that economies where price per unit goes down as more items are produced (as a result of production processes) are actually very rare. Instead, size does seem to be important where networks and grids are the basis of the business, such as in telephone and utility industries.

From looking at the size of businesses in different cultures, it appears that when you have removed the economies of scale due to promotion and networks, the remaining determinant of price efficiency is the effectiveness of the communication mechanisms in providing useful and reliable information.

In Japan there are many firms so large that they dwarf anything elsewhere in similar businesses: for example, the trading companies Mitsubishi and Mitsui. Japan also has giant businesses, such as Nikon and Yamaha boats, that totally depend on people who work at home. Both exist because of the homogeneity of the Japanese people, and the extraordinarily effective communication mechanism that arises from the familylike relations among the 120 million people on those small islands. It is a very tight family; foreign visitors often observe that there are no business secrets in Japan.

A few giant firms that are not in production or network industries are to be found in West Germany. West Germany also has a very cohesive, homogeneous population with reliable social communication mechanisms. On the other hand, Chinese companies in Singapore, Taiwan and Hong Kong seldom reach a large scale because management in each business is always limited to the size of the *family* that owns the business. In these cultures, outsiders are never trusted enough to be brought into the tight inner circle of management communication.

The size of a business is generally determined by the effectiveness of its communications mechanisms, other things being equal. The thesis of this book is that openness in business results in a more effective mechanism of communication.

How Big?

Returning to the question, "How big can honest business grow?" the answer is: Starting from scratch, it has the potential for growing much larger than a nonhonest, or secretive business in the same industry. The reason is that a larger number of people can work together as the level of mutual trust increases. The greater the openness of the honest business, the greater the potential for trust.

"Starting from scratch" is an important prerequisite to this statement. In Western cultures, the tradition of secrecy and self-aggrandizement is too strong to allow existing businesses to make wholesale conversions to open, honest practices. Therefore, it is necessary to start from scratch with new businesses, incorporating openness and honesty every day, at every decision juncture. The businesses that the authors have worked with have started with these operating practices and, if they continue, and grow carefully, paying minute attention to the effects and methods of openness and honesty, we can expect to see a new class of businesses emerge. They will be strategically more effective and larger than their peers. Larger, for us, means involving more people in a coordinated direction; the specific form of new honest businesses may not be the traditional corporate enterprise.

We believe the future will include an increasing number of honest businesses, large and small. We don't expect the businesses that grow large will take the form of large businesses that are currently found in the marketplace. There are already forces operating in the United States to scale down many types of businesses; quite a few large chain stores are failing, and more will do so. Based on Japanese evidence, we expect small independent businesses in a number of fields to out-perform large chains. Such fields include all instances where service, customization and local supplies are important. These are clothing, food, housing and nearly all social services. The fields specifically include bakeries, groceries, shoe stores, apparel goods and furniture stores, at the expense of Macy's, Sears, Safeway, Woolworth's, Hertz and Hilton. The superior communications mechanisms that have given these large companies advantages of scale will be offset by improved communication networks within these industries, as honest practices are introduced by smaller businesses, who will form supportive associations. One prototype is the garment industry with its small, independent businesses established on the basis of quality products, reliability and flexibility.

Applying New Practices

There are many ways in which existing large businesses can adopt elements of honest business practices. The simplest is to open all of their files, reports, record keeping information, etc., to everyone. In day-to-day terms, this must be done slowly so that the individual employees have time to adjust to the new operating environment, or to leave. If every major opening of information segments is done over a period of a year, with adequate notice to everyone concerned, then employees have time to accommodate their behavior to the new expectations. For example, the act of opening all personnel files, including wages, should require one year's notice to all concerned. Many supervisors would need a year's time to equalize wages among subordinates in instances where differentials couldn't be defended publicly. Similarly, many personal social problems, like alcoholism, might surface, which would require developing supportive management programs in lieu of ignoring the issue.

Opening up internal information segments will allow many techniques discussed in the Management chapter to be applied.

Much of the information in the chapter on Community can be of use in traditional businesses. We have worked with traditional businesses that were able to incorporate some of the practices described here. One such business was a medium-sized woolen mill in England that had a long history of good labor relations, had a product that was priced 20 percent higher than its competitors, and was very susceptible to great fluctuations in the general economy. They were considering a variety of strategies to broaden their market and change products. Working with our understanding of community, they were able to see the connection between themselves and their customers. They have explored three practices that didn't require a major change in their way of doing business, and stabilized the demand for their woven wool. First, they have reduced their use of sales representatives, and increased direct sales to final users all over the world, so they'll know their customers personally. Second, having this direct relationship with the final customer, they are doing much more custom work, which includes freelance work on the part of some of their employees. Third, they have established very close relations between their own employees and the employees of their customer companies. Customers now phone directly to the production-line employees at the woolen mill and discuss fiber content and color problems, and are establishing close friendship networks. In the future, it is expected that the friendship and customizing elements in the business will result in greater stability of customer orders and sales.

The range of opportunities to use the community of a business is extensive. We have worked with banks that developed programs to bring their own business customers into greater contact with each other; and with government agencies that formed monthly panels of employees, selected randomly to meet personally with top management and to open new channels of information.

Implications of Honest Business in the World Markets

There is overwhelming evidence that the practices of honest business are strategically superior to traditional business styles. It is also evident that the innovativeness and vitality that the U.S. has prided itself on in the past are not currently effective in the world market in comparison with Japan, Korea, West Germany and Singapore. Other cultures that are old and homogeneous are adapting to high technology and complex production systems with great effectiveness. What can heterogeneous cultures like the U.S. do?

The answer is develop more openness. The broadest useful and agreed-upon evidence is that open Western societies continue to be more commercially productive than Iron Curtain countries that are closed and secretive. This evidence suggests that greater openness, not only in our society, but in our business practices as well, is important.

The special connection between honest business practices and openness in other areas, government practices in particular, is visible in the life of I. F. Stone. To many people, Stone is one of the greatest journalists in American history, the man who single-handedly created modern methods of investigative journalism, who first exposed the roots of the Vietnam War and became the spiritual leader of the Watergate investigation. To us, he is a great example of an honest, open businessperson.

Isador F. Stone was a concentration camp survivor, who came to the U.S. after the Second World War, when the country was open to refugees. Stone started a newsletter business. He began with a small subscription list in the early 1950s, made up of people who had read various magazine columns he wrote from 1947 to 1951. Living and publishing on the $5 per year subscriptions revenues from his original five thousand person mailing list, he put out a four-page weekly letter of news and opinion. He rarely hired others to work for him, loyally stuck with one printer for twenty years, lived in Washington, D.C., with his wife in a modest home, and always put the newsletters in the mailbox himself. I. F. Stone created a solid business that grew to over 100,000 subscribers in the late 1960s. During all the years that he ran his newsletter business, there was never advertising, promoting or deliberate efforts to grow bigger. Word of mouth was his only source of new customers. Stone overcame carcinoma and worked for years with partial blindness while publishing his newsletter.

Stone was effective as an innovator in investigative journalism because of his independent personal business. As an employee, he would have been fired or pressured time and again until he became subservient. Relying on his independent business status, he was able to create a community of readers who were his financial supporters. His career is an example of the role of an open business practice in an open society.

We believe that greater openness at every level of government, business and personal life of American society will result in greater potential for cooperation, will decrease the level of factionalism over several decades and will rapidly result in greater productivity and innovativeness. These conclusions are drawn directly from our experience in dealing with open, honest business.

C. Facts About This Book and the Authors

The typeface used in this book is Garamond. The layout was suggested by the authors and designed by Bernard Klein of Random House. The photographs were done by Michael, Rasberry, Carole Rae and Mush Emmons.

This book is copublished by Clear Glass Publishing and Random House. Clear Glass Publishing is a name and a bank account that represents the partnership between Michael and Rasberry, and has a contract with Random House. Copublishing is a joint venture between two companies. Books are sold by the publisher to retail stores at a published discount rate that ranges, depending on the number purchased, for hardcover, from about 25 percent to about 46 percent; for paperback, about 45 to 46 percent: and sold to wholesalers, for hardcover, from about 46 to 48 percent; for paperback, from about 46 to 50 percent.

Of the amount received from the customer, Random House and Clear Glass share expenses such as distribution, advertising and promotion, the cost of producing the book, overhead and royalties to the author. Rasberry and Michael receive royalties of 7.5 percent to 30,000 copies, 9 percent to 50,000 copies and 10 percent thereafter. After all these costs are subtracted from what is collected from the customer, Random House and Clear Glass share the profits or losses equally.

Michael and Rasberry wrote *The Seven Laws of Money*, which was published in 1974. They edited and wrote the Introduction to *The Briarpatch Book*, which was published by New Glide in 1978, and worked on *Honest Business* from January 1978 to May 1980. Most of the time, writing was done two days a week, when Rasberry commuted to San Francisco from her home in Bodega Bay where she lives on a large sheep ranch. All the sections on individual business people in the book were submitted to the people mentioned, and their permission was obtained. The book was shown to over fifteen people whose judgments were valued. Of these fifteen, many were very helpful, and two were very influential. Special gratitude goes to Peter Sherrill and Dick Raymond. Peter taught a course in "The Structure of Rational Knowledge" for both of the authors, and introduced the concept of business as transactions. Peter also encouraged greater rigor in the concepts used in the book. Dick Raymond read an early draft of the book that used the term "entrepreneur" frequently. Dick convinced the authors that "entrepreneur" was a vague word which did not accurately communicate a sound concept. This lead to the development of the concept of tradeskills and to a chapter on that subject.

Editing of the book was done by Charlotte Mayerson at Random House. Charlotte is a close friend of both authors, and wrote nearly forty pages of insightful and powerful editorial comment, most of which was incorporated. The authors wanted her editorial comments included as footnotes, but were convinced by Charlotte that it would be distracting to the reader.

We would also like to acknowledge the persistance, dedication and hard work that Shali Parsons, Bahauddin Alpine and Annie Stryon have given to the Briarpatch Network. Thanks to Joe Mancuso and the American Management Association.

Michael Phillips, forty-one years old at the time this book was published, lives in San Francisco. He was an undergraduate at the University of Chicago and a graduate student in Economics at the University of California at Berkeley. During his twenties Michael was a banker with the Bank of America and the Bank of California. At age thirty, he was made a vice-president of the Bank of California. He introduced simplified checking account systems on a wide scale to California banking and, as is often true in banking, the ideas quickly spread throughout the country. He was a key organizer of Mastercharge (now called Mastercard), the bank credit card that is owned and operated by an association of banks. He developed the first consumer savings certificates of deposit in the late 1960s, and developed the modern concepts of corporate cash management, which he taught to other bankers and to the corporate treasurers of many major American companies. In the 1970s Michael was president of Point Foundation, and business manager of Glide Memorial United Methodist Church. As president of Point, he funded many projects related to corporate social responsibility, and helped to organize many proxy fights against major U.S. companies on social issues. As manager of Glide, he administers an investment fund of $6 million, managed a 250-room major hotel, and operates office buildings and several small businesses. From the early 1970s, he has worked with over seven hundred small businesses in the San Francisco Bay Area, helping them start, grow, merge, sell and go out of business. Of these, more than four hundred fifty were active in the network of small businesses that Michael helped to found, called the Briarpatch Network, and called by its members "a network of friends in business."

Rasberry, thirty-nine at the time this book was published, lives and works on a sheep ranch north of San Francisco. Rasberry coauthored and copublished the classic *Rasberry Exercises: How to Start Your Own School and Make Your Own Book.* Her background includes community organizing, independent press publishing and film making. Rasberry, well noted for her iron-fisted control of her co-author, lives the concepts upon which this book is based, but has no formal business training. Her role as midwife to *Honest Business* was so important that she is a fifty percent partner.

PARTNERSHIP AGREEMENT
between
Michael Phillips and Salli Rasberry

This partnership shall be called Clear Glass Publishing.

Michael and Rasberry are writing *Honest Business* together as they like to collaborate. They have worked together on a film; Michael provided funds and support for a film festival Rasberry orchestrated; they wrote the Introduction together for *The Briarpatch Book*; and published, edited, designed and wrote the successful *The Seven Laws of Money.* They love each other and have fun together. They have been friends for nine years.

Rasberry and Michael are splitting the work and profits on the book *Honest Business* 50–50. The partnership shall handle accounting with checks to be mailed to each separately.

Part of their responsibility as authors includes any revisions and updates on future editions, if any. A major responsibility is answering mail, granting interviews, traveling to other cities for TV and radio shows, writing articles related to *Honest Business* and, in general, marketing the book.

If at some point after January 1, 1985, one person is clearly responsible for the book, Rasberry and Michael shall meet and if they do not divide the work equitably, the percentage of the partnership income in subsequent reprints shall reflect that fact and shall be changed, with 75 percent going to the person now responsible and 25 percent going to the inactive partner.

Should Rasberry and Michael disagree on this partnership agreement, Peter Sherill and Bahauddin Alpine shall be asked to arbitrate. Their consensus agreement is binding. If these men are unavailable, two other peers from within the community as listed on Attachment A, shall be selected.

Rasberry likes receiving mail and feedback and requests that Michael copy all letters and articles that come his way as a result of *Honest Business* so she may share in this reward. She will also share same with him.

Upon completion of the book Rasberry and Michael should meet twice a month to review remaining work and to avoid one person becoming responsible for the book.

Buy-out: Either partner shall be able to buy the other's share for a price equal to or less than the previous two years' total of that person's royalty times three.

Death: Rights shall go to the estate of each partner.

Signed:

Michael Phillips
Salli Rasberry

Attachment A

Dick Baker Roshi
Stewart Brand
Winnie McIlvenna
Dick Raymond
Charlotte Mayerson

INDEX

abandonment of businesses, 135
accountants, accounting, 8, 73, 127–
    128
    see also books
accrual system, 75
advertising and promotion, ix, 40,
    63–64, 128–131, 133–134
    fun and, 123–124
    McDonald's use of, 55–56
    of publications, 24, 25, 31–34
    see also publicity
Albert, Charles, 132
Albini, Pete, 173
Alpine, Bahauddin, 25, 123–124
American Arbitration Association,
    150, 155
American Telephone and Telegraph
    Co. (AT&T), 93–94, 175
answering machines, need for, 7
anxiety, coping with, 131–132
apprentices, 132–133
arbitration, litigation vs., 150
artists in business, 133–134
assets, concern for, 8
Avis marketing campaign, 58

Bair, Bess, 17, 125, 133–134
Balance Sheets, 74, 76
bank loans, 49, 74, 78
    collateral for, 138
    to corporations, 146
    co-signers of, 138
    description of application for,
        138–139
    S.B.A. as guarantor of, 165
    when to apply for, 138
Bank of America, 175, 176–177
    Saturday openings of, 67–68
bankruptcy, 135, 136–137
    withholding tax liability and,
        147–148
banks, banking, 49, 137–139, 196
    barter, 139
    branch, 175, 176
    language of, 138
    volatile nature of, 74
barter, 139–140
    for overdue bills, 141
Bell Laboratories, 175, 181–182
Better Business Bureau (BBB), 140
bills:
    overdue, collection of, 141–142

bills (*continued*)
    prompt payment of, 101–103
    trading of, 141–142
Bluestone, Irving, 116–117
board of directors, outsiders on, 109, 110
Bolivar experiment, 109, 116–118
bookkeepers, advice from, 73
books, 71–90
    management affected by, 105
    open, 83–90, 105
    as taboo, 72
Brand, Stewart, 16, 47
    open books used by, 85–86
Briarpatch Book, The, 53–55, 56–58
business(es):
    closing of, 135–137
    definition and characteristics of, 3–9
    examining motives for being in, 167–168
    failure of, xi, 11, 13, 40, 43, 155
    history of, 183–192
    loving of, 23–27
    minimum time for starting of, 23
business ability, tradeskill vs., 11
businesses, honest:
    concept of, ix–xi
    implications in world markets of, 197–198
    size of, 193, 195
businesses, large:
    adopting honest business practices in, 195–196
    cluster of businesses vs., 193–194

capital, small, 43–50
    benefits of, 44–48
    defined, 48–49
cash accounting, 75
cash flow, defined, 151
Chambers of Commerce, variability in, 141

charities, business vs., 8
checkbook register, classification used in, 73
Chickering, Sherman, 123–124
collectives, management of, 118–119
communication, 59–60
    business management and, 105–106
    in large vs. small businesses, 193–194
    in nonprofit businesses, 26
    see also advertising and promotion; publicity
Communion Restaurant, 85
    complete vision of, 53–55, 58
community, 7, 93–98
    advertising in, 129
    barter and, 140
    components of, 94
    loans from, 49
    management affected by, 105
    open books and growth of, 85–86
    Penney stores as concerned with, 179–180
    traditional businesses making use of, 196
Community Services Administration, 143
Conlon, Tom, 24, 63–64
consignment, final sales vs., 152
consultants, pensions and, 158
contracts:
    Bolivar "shelter agreement" as, 116–117
    for personal situations, 13, 97–98
cooperatives, 143
Copperfield, David, 25
copyrights, 142–143
corporations, 143–146
    advantages of, 145
    alternatives to, 143–145
    introduction of, 192
    myths about, 146

nonprofit, 152–154
scientific research at, 175, 181–
182
costs:
of materials, 75
overhead, 48, 151
of patents, 157
per unit of product, 79
reduction of, 16, 160–161
courts, small claims, 166
Crafts Business Encyclopedia, The
(Scott), 151
credit cards, 146–147
creditors:
liquidation and, 136
loans in payment of, 138
open books appreciated by, 84–85
Crumb, Robert, copyright case of,
143
customers, 68
copyright confusion and, 143
factors affecting decisions of, 45,
46, 60, 72
quality control and surveys of,
163–164
service of, 37–41, 46
sex with, 164

Dakin, Henry, 6
days off, determining right time for,
76–77
details, attention to, 44–46
De Woody, George, 167–168
direct-mail-order campaign, 130
Dodson, Betty, 33–34
Drucker, Peter F., 107–108, 120
Durham, Louie, 118

Ebla, business practices in, 190–192
employees, 40
for management role, 109–113
open books and, 83, 85
partnership among, 89, 178

pension plans for, 158
periodic review of, 106–107
responsibility assumed by, 18, 113
sex with, 164
in small capital businesses, 48
supervision of, 113–119
tax criteria for, 148
unions and, 166–167
wages of, ix, 26, 48, 136
withholding tax on, 88–89, 147–
148
energy, focusing of, 29–35
equipment:
financing of, 138
in partnerships, 155
renting of, 171
*Everybody's Guide to Small Claims
Court,* 166
exchanges, transactions vs., 4–5
exclusive rights, 148–149

facing the facts, as attribute of
tradeskill, 14, 15–16, 19
family, 96
in development of tradeskill, 11–
14, 20
monetary needs of, 169, 172
size of business and, 194
written agreements with, 97–98
Federal Bureau of Investigation
(FBI), 87–88
financial statements, 74–80, 83
guessing at nature of businesses
from, 78–79
loan application and, 139
timeliness of, 80
financing, *see* bank loans; loans
five-and-a-half-day work week,
initiation of, 175, 177
fixed price retailing, 160, 192
focus in business, importance of, 29–
35
Follett, Robert, 128

Franklin, Ben, 157–158
FRAP (Flat Response Audio Pick-
   up), 87, 101–102
fraud, x–xi, 5
freedom, money as, 169, 170–171
Freeman, Andora, 38–39, 169*n*
French, Richard, 129
friends, 96
   acquiring possessions from, 171
   bankers as, 137
   loans from, 49
   pricing and, 159
   written agreements with, 13, 97–
      98
full employment plan (Procter &
   Gamble), 178
fun, business as, 26, 123–126

Germany, West, business communication in, 194
Giannini, Amadeo Peter, 109, 175,
   176–177
   accessibility of, 58–59
Gnaizda, Bob, 38
going slow, as rational business
   strategy, 63–68, 130
Gordon, Richie, 111–112
government, in financing of business,
   49
Granary, The, 71–72
Green Gulch Greengrocer, complete
   vision of, 56–58

hands-on learning, as attribute of
   tradeskill, 14, 17–18, 19
Hargadon, Tom, 95–96
Harmon, Sidney, 116–117
Harmon Industries, innovative man-
   agement experiment by, 116–
   118
Hawken, Paul, 18
Hecht, Joy, 38–39
hobbies, business vs., 7

Hoge, C. C., Sr., 130–131
Hohenstein, Nan, 103
Hurwich, Rudy, 25–27

ideas, completeness of, 53–60
illness, expenses and, 75
income, business, 74–78
   future, 139
   sources of, 77–78
Income/Expense Sheet, 74–76
   pricing and, 159
independent contractors, 147–148
innovation, in small capital businesses, 46–47
Internal Revenue Service (IRS), 6, 8
   open books and, 87–89
   Special Services Section (SSS)
      and, 87–88
   withholding tax and, 147–148
   see also taxes
inventory, 49, 74, 138
invoices, 151

Japan, giant businesses in, 194
Johnson, Huey, 40–41

Kadish, Morrie, 39–40
Kahn, Bob, 163
Kammaroff, Bernard (Bear), 31–32,
   128
Keogh pension plans, 158–159
Koontz, Harold, 120

lawyers, 127, 149–150
   partnerships and, 156
   patents and, 157
liquidation of businesses, 135–137,
   145
Living Together Kit, The (Shara and
   Warner), 97–98
loans, 48, 49, 84, 97
   bank, *see* bank loans

home, 176
from S.B.A., 165–166

McDonald's, complete vision of, 55–56
Macoby, Michael, 116–118
Macy, Barry, 117
maintenance, 48
management, 18, 105–120, 196
  as communication, 105–106
  courses on, 106
  further reading on, 120
  outside advisory on, 109, 110–112
  structural openness of, 108–119
Management (Drucker), 107–108
Manning, Mimi, 134
Margolin, Malcolm, 183–190
market:
  capital and pressures of, 45
  community vs., 94
marketing, complete ideas vs., 58
marketing plans, 150–151
media, 161–163
  advertising and, 129–130
  requirements for dealing with, 162
memo, shipping on, 151–152
mergers, 135
money, four illusions of, 158, 167, 169–174
muddles, as business organizations, 143, 144
Murray, Peter, 94

Near, Gary, 38
negotiation, as alternative to lawyer, 150
nonprofit businesses, 26, 152–154
  types of, 152

Ohlone Way, The (Margolin), 183–190
old age, preparing for, 158–159, 172–174

openness, as characteristic of honest business, ix–xi, 83–90, 105
overhead, long-term, 48

paintings, as nonmonetary Keogh plan, 158–159
parentalism, as bad management practice, 115
partnership, 13, 143, 145, 154–156
  complexity as suited to, 156
  among employees, 89, 178
  family, 97
  general, 145, 146, 154, 155
  limited, 145, 146, 154–155
  Phillips-Rasberry agreement, 201–202
  store, 175, 180
  verbal, 154
patents, 156–158
  problems with, 157
Peavey, Frances, 34–35, 64, 65, 103
Penney, James Cash, 109, 175, 178–180
pension plans, 158–159, 177
  corporations and, 145
persistence, as attribute of tradeskill, 14–15, 19
Person, Bob, 128
personalized barter, benefits of, 139–140
PERT Charting, 106
Philips Corporation, 149
Phillips, Carole, 46
Phillips, Wendell, 14, 172–173
Point Foundation, 110
postal rates, 153
pricing, ix, 53–54, 57, 194
  of businesses, 135
  determination of, 159
  fixed vs. negotiated, 160
Procter, William Cooper, 109, 175, 177–178
production, PERT Charting in, 106

product liability insurance, 161
profit-sharing plans, pioneering of, 175, 178
publicity, 161–163
  disadvantages of, 161–162
  by word of mouth, 25, 128, 162
publishing:
  costs in, 16
  distribution and, 24, 25, 30–34, 123–124

quality control, 108, 163–164

Rae, Carole, 38, 103, 125
Raymond, Dick, 18
RCA, exclusive approach used by, 149
receipts, daily, 73
regularity over time, as element in business, 6–8
rent, 48, 138
respect, money as source of, 167, 169, 171–172
restaurants, 24–25, 64
  capital requirements and, 43–44, 46, 47, 48
  completeness of ideas and, 53–56, 58, 59–60
  fun in, 126
  openness in, x–xi
  quality control of, 163
retirement, 159, 172–174
risks:
  banks uninterested in, 138
  minimizing of, 14, 17, 19–20, 161
Rugge, Sue, 41

Safeway, independents vs., 193–194
sales:
  of businesses, 135
  records of, 73, 77, 78
  vital ratios and, 151

San Andreas Health Council, 110–112
Schwartz, Bob, 13–14
Scientology, Church of, 108
Scott, M., 151
security:
  as employee concern, 167, 178
  money as, 167, 169, 172–174
service:
  bartering of, 171
  credit cards as, 147
  poor, 40, 46
  as primary goal of businesses, 37–41
service marks, 142–143
sex, in small businesses, 164–165
Small Business Administration (S.B.A.):
  loans from, 165–166
  programs created by, 166
Small Business Investment Corp. (S.B.I.C.), 165, 166
small claims court, 166
Smith, Tom, 41
social security, nonprofit businesses and, 153
sole proprietorship, 143, 144–145
  liability suits and, 146
  tax schedule for, 144
State Corporation Commissioner, 144
Stewart, Alexander, 160
Stone, Isador F., 197
Strong, Earl P., 120
Styron, Annie, 57
Sub-Chapter S form, 146

Taft-Hartley Act, 166
Tatum, Don, 19
taxes:
  advantages for co-ops in, 143
  corporations and, 145, 146, 152–154
  employees and, 88–89, 147–148

nonmonetary Keogh plans and, 158–159
partnership and, 145
sole proprietorship and, 144, 145
Tax Reform Act (1969), 152
teaching, pensions and, 158
timing, 63–68
of business openings, 64–65
toy recycling businesses, 38–39, 64–65
trade marks and trade names, 142–143
trade secrecy, open books and, 86–87
tradeskill, 11–20, 161
attributes of, 14–20
parents and childhood experience in development of, 11–14, 20
special training for, 13
transactions, 3–6
business as series of, 6

unions, ix, 166–167
utilities, 48, 74, 138

vacations, 75
finding time for, 76–77
need for, 109, 113
Vail, Theodore N., 109, 175, 180–182
vital ratios, defined, 151

wages, ix, 48
in nonprofit businesses, 26
voluntary liquidation and, 136
Wall Street Journal, 135
Warne, Gary, 124
window dressing, 74

Yellow Pages, 131